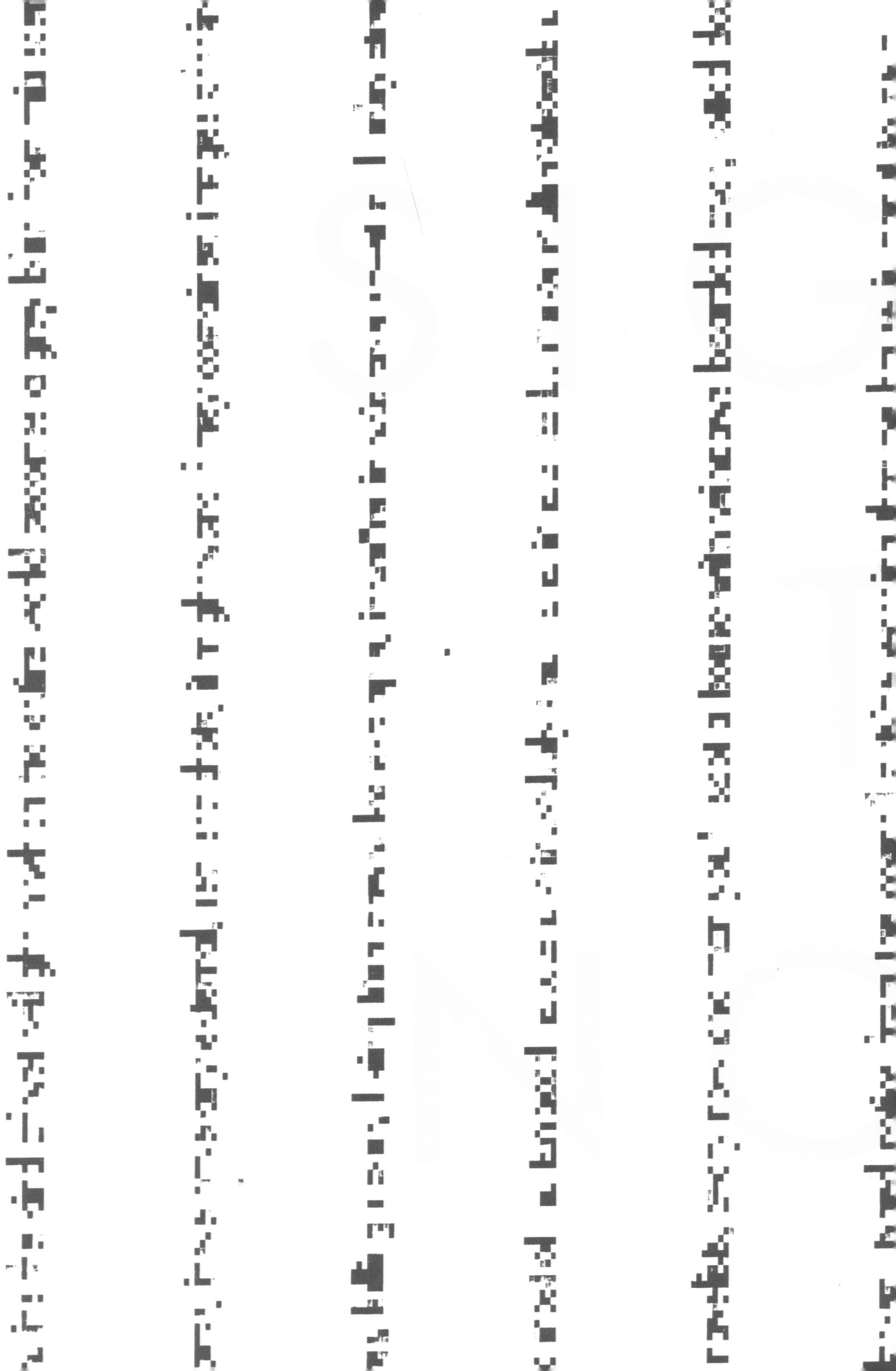

WRITTEN

BY

NEIL GAIMAN

ILLUSTRATED

AND

DESIGNED

BY

DAVE McKEAN

First published in
Great Britain 1992
in VG Graphics
by Victor Gollancz Ltd.

First published in the
United States 1992 by
Dark Horse Comics, Inc.

Dark Horse Comics, Inc.
10956 Main Street
Milwaukie, OR 97222

Second edition
Second printing

U.S. ISBN 1-56971-144-5

Printed and bound in
Hong Kong by Imago
Publishing Ltd.

DEDICATIONS

Neil: This one's for Emma Bull and Will Shetterly. And Fourth Street.

Dave: To Rolie Green, for giving myself, Clare and the film director your warmth and humour.

ACKNOWLEDGEMENTS

Neil: Thanks to Sheryl Garratt and Phil Bicker at The Face, who asked us for a comic strip; to Faith Brooker who gave the end result a good home. Thanks also to Archie Goodwin (who tried), to Merrilee Heifetz and Carole Blake.

Dave: To Rolie Green and Cathy Peters. To Splash of Paint Design for facilities. To John, Marian and Anne at Kall Kwik, Camberley for patience, and Barron Storey for hard criticism.

INTRODUCTION BY JONATHAN CARROLL

When I was a teacher, one of the first things I would tell students at the beginning of any year was never, ever read

the introduction before you've read the novel. For some perverse reason, the introducer invariably tells you the plot

('After Anna Karenina throws herself in front of the train . . .'), or talks about characters and situations you are

unfamiliar with because, wonder of wonders, you haven't read the story yet.

Because I have the highest respect for Gaiman and McKean, I offer instead an invisible introduction. You can read it

and not worry about the above. Up front I tell you it is only an appreciation of the work of two people who are doing

something both dangerous and necessary. Like heart surgeons, astronauts, like new lovers.

Collaborations are difficult and treacherous. More so when you have a number of genuinely original sensibilities working on a single product. The only problem I have with the work of these men is both are so good at what they do

that I often find myself reading and not looking, or vice versa. That is unfair because a tale like SIGNAL TO NOISE

demands the reader take everything in at once before moving on. All the words that cut to the quick and the ominous,

all the unprecedented images that are a kind of hieroglyphics of the now. Compare it to the old stereopticon. Alone

you have a card with 'only' two pictures. Slipped into the gizmo and viewed correctly, you have magic, vision beyond

the ordinary.

Vision is the key word here. Not noise. The title itself is a contradiction because today we are surrounded by so much

noise that it is virtually impossible to detect any signals whatsoever in it. And even if we were somehow able to work

our way through, then find or recognize the true signals, would we know how to respond? What is the point of a quest

if we're unable to recognize the goal even when we come to it? I will cheat a little here and tell you this: SIGNAL TO

NOISE is about a filmmaker who, on learning he has a fatal disease, decides nevertheless to continue working on a

project until his last day. What are we to make of this? Mankind's indomitable spirit? Or the ugly flipside – life's a

bitch and then you die? The quest is best, or any quest is a bust?

The critic Robert Harbison has said 'True guidebooks should lead you to things and leave you at the door, lists of

places where certain kinds of experiences may be had. If you are reading you cannot see, and the other way around.

Travelers should read only after dark.' (Robert Harbison, *Eccentric Spaces*). What is astonishing to me is that virtuosos

like McKean and Gaiman do both. They lead you there, then take you through showing you what to look for. They

may well be creating the ultimate 'guidebooks' for our quest and our time, the necessary ones.

Much has been written recently about how comics have grown up, but that is a serious misnomer. From the beginning,

the intention of comics was to entertain. SIGNAL TO NOISE does not entertain. It scratches, it provokes, it frightens. It tells you things you don't want to know but then twists you inside out by saying, look harder and see the poignance,

the beauty of light dancing on life's edge, truth that is as simple and direct as death. It is not a 'comic'. It is not an

'illustrated novel', the going term these days which unfortunately always smacks to me of those sexy magazines you

see vacant eye'd people reading on public buses in Italy or Spain. I wish someone would dig deeper and come up with

a right name for them.

Because at their best, experiencing these works is like a month spent in the high Alps. You return thinner, stronger.

You've grown accustomed to silence and thus learned of an inner voice which has been talking, urgent but unheard, a

long time. You have less patience now with the white noise of the world, but that will work to your advantage.

Early in this story, a doctor tells the dying man 'You've got to let us examine you. You've got to let us treat you.' He

demurs, but anyone who reads SIGNAL TO NOISE has already begun treatment.

"EVERYTHING HAS A MEANING OR NOTHING HAS. TO PUT IT ANOTHER WAY, ONE COULD SAY THAT ART IS WITHOUT NOISE."

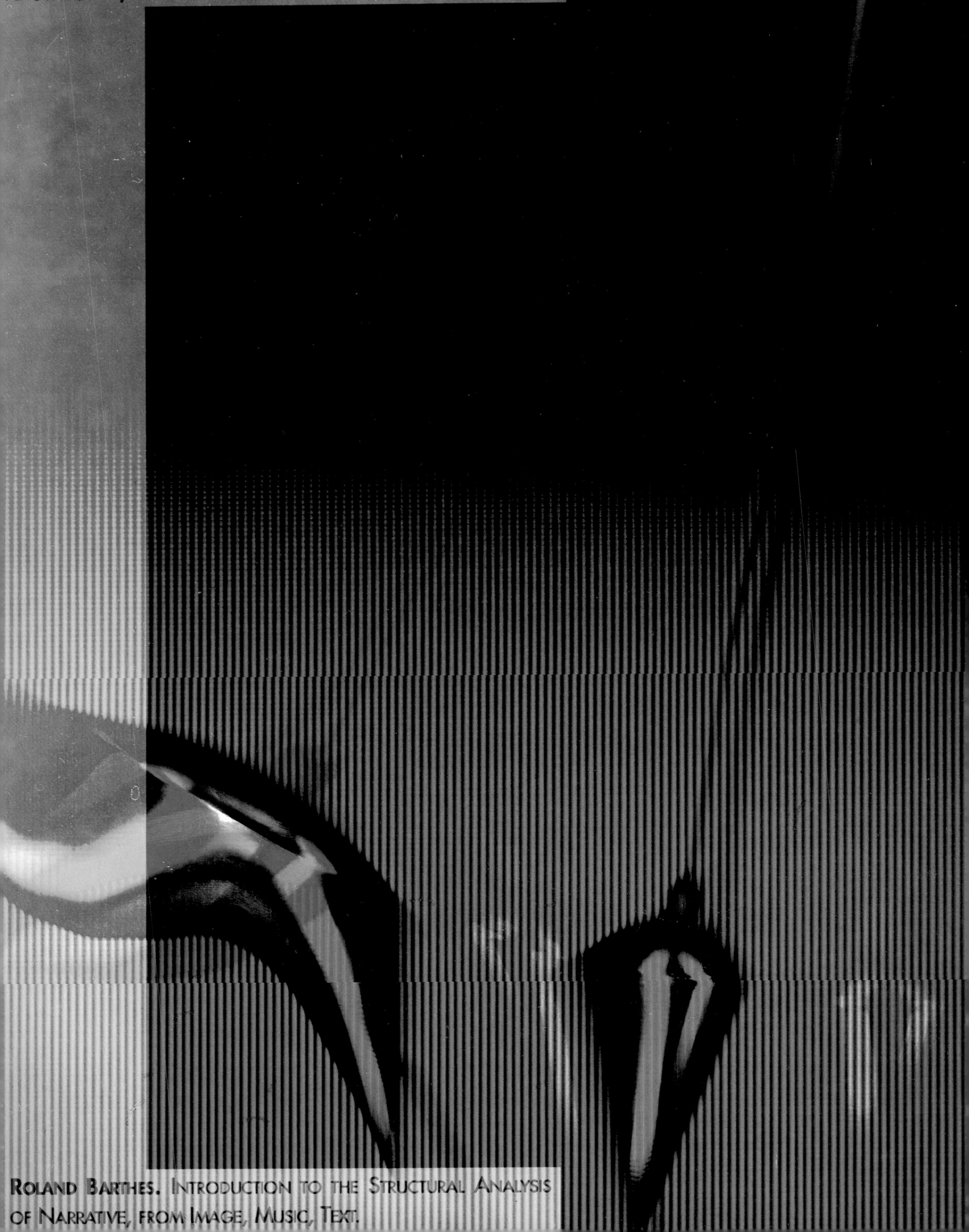

ROLAND BARTHES. INTRODUCTION TO THE STRUCTURAL ANALYSIS OF NARRATIVE, FROM IMAGE, MUSIC, TEXT.

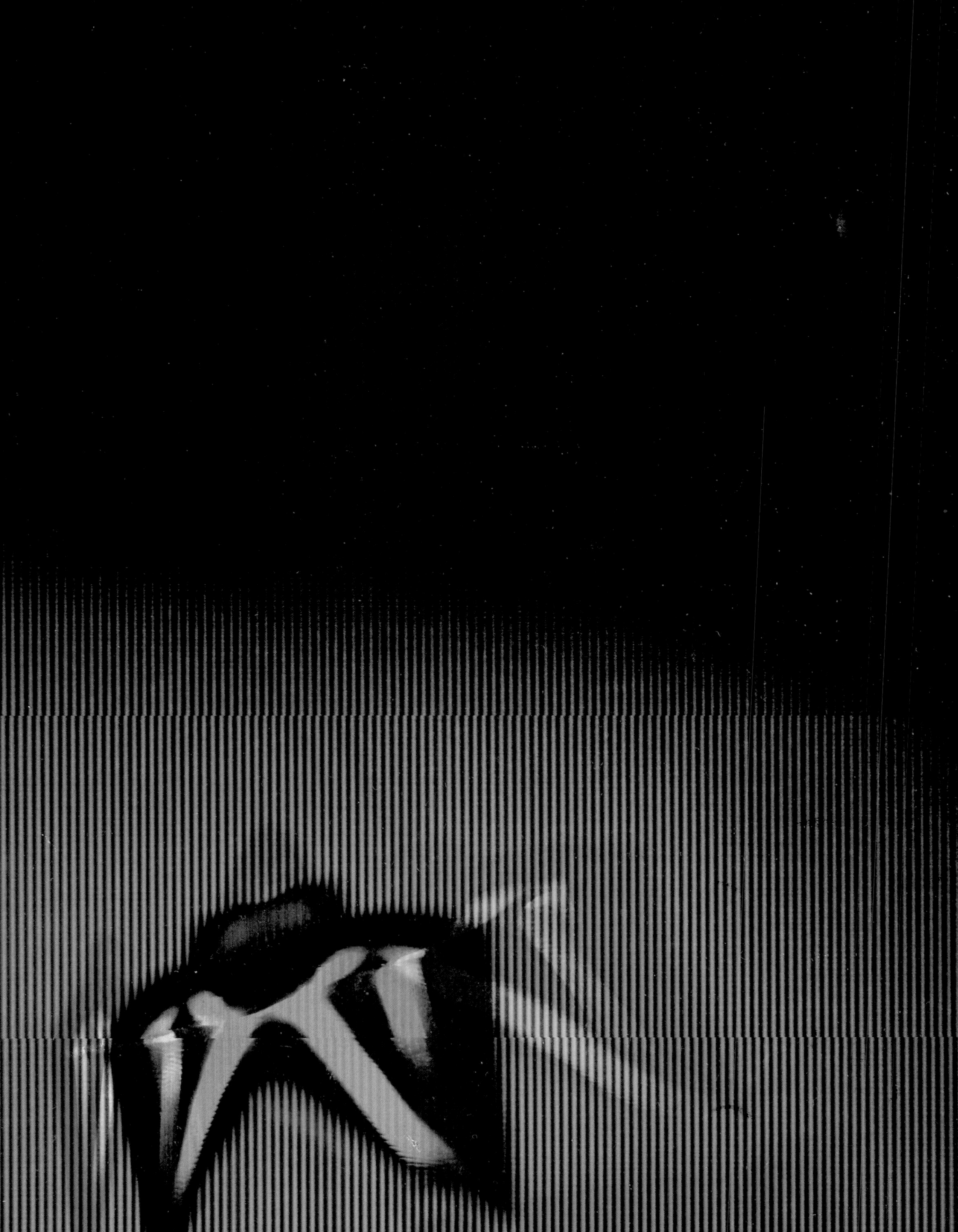

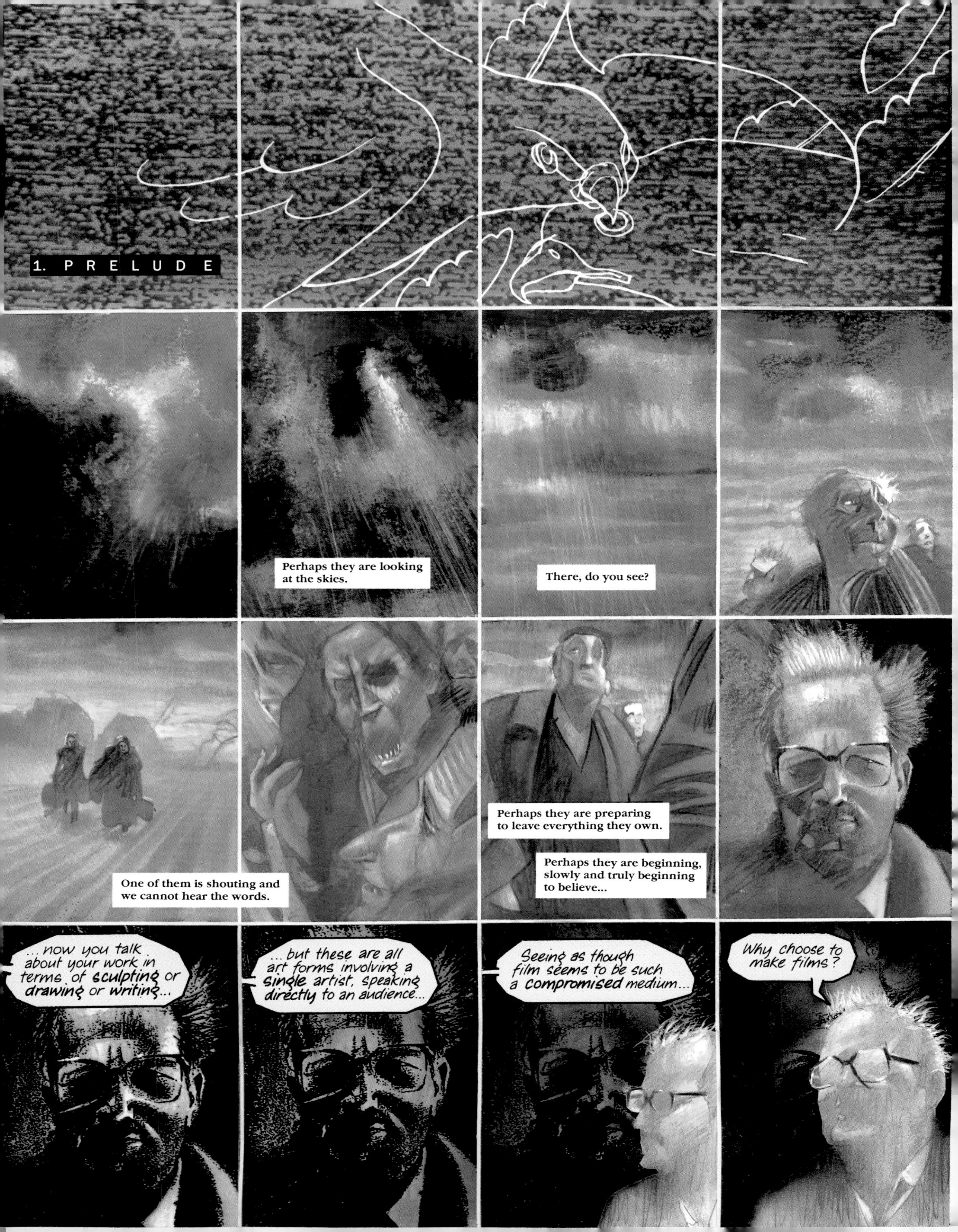
1. PRELUDE
Perhaps they are looking at the skies.
There, do you see?
One of them is shouting and we cannot hear the words.
Perhaps they are preparing to leave everything they own.
Perhaps they are beginning, slowly and truly beginning to believe...
...now you talk about your work in terms of sculpting or drawing or writing...
...but these are all art forms involving a single artist, speaking directly to an audience...
Seeing as though film seems to be such a compromised medium...
Why choose to make films?

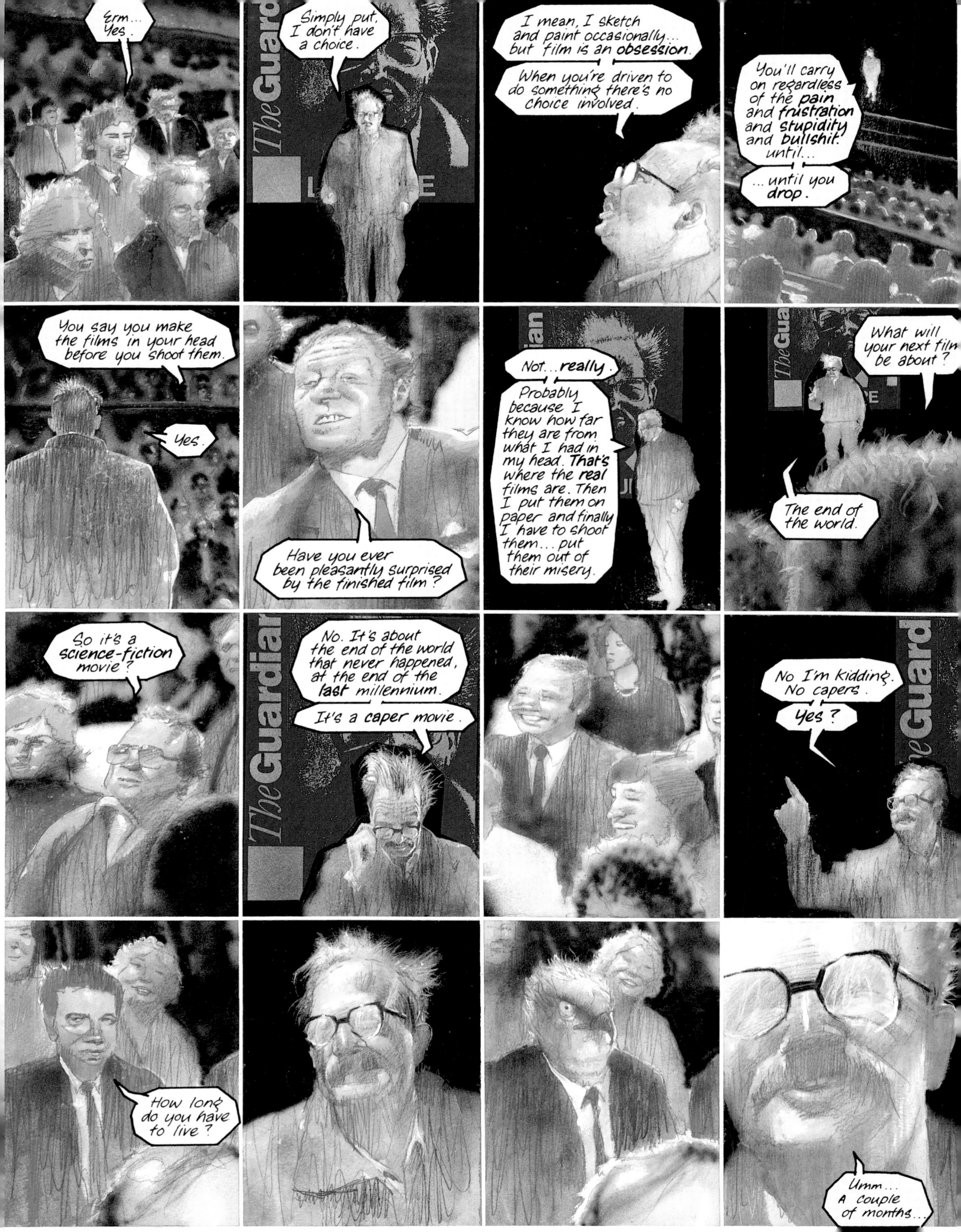
Erm... Yes.
Simply put, I don't have a choice.
I mean, I sketch and paint occasionally... but film is an obsession.
When you're driven to do something there's no choice involved.
You'll carry on regardless of the pain and frustration and stupidity and bullshit. until...
...until you drop.
You say you make the films in your head before you shoot them.
Yes.
Have you ever been pleasantly surprised by the finished film?
Not... really.
Probably because I know how far they are from what I had in my head. That's where the real films are. Then I put them on paper and finally I have to shoot them... put them out of their misery.
What will your next film be about?
The end of the world.
So it's a science-fiction movie?
No. It's about the end of the world that never happened, at the end of the last millennium.
It's a caper movie.
No I'm kidding. No capers.
Yes?
How long do you have to live?
Umm... A couple of months...

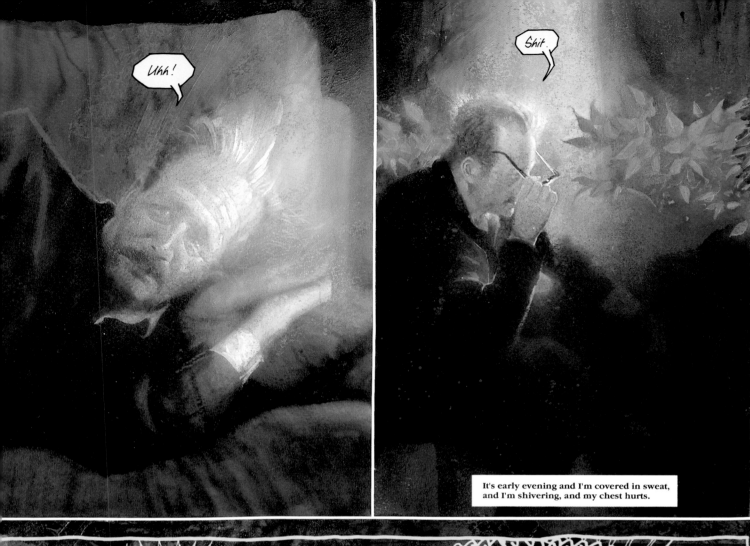

It's early evening and I'm covered in sweat, and I'm shivering, and my chest hurts.

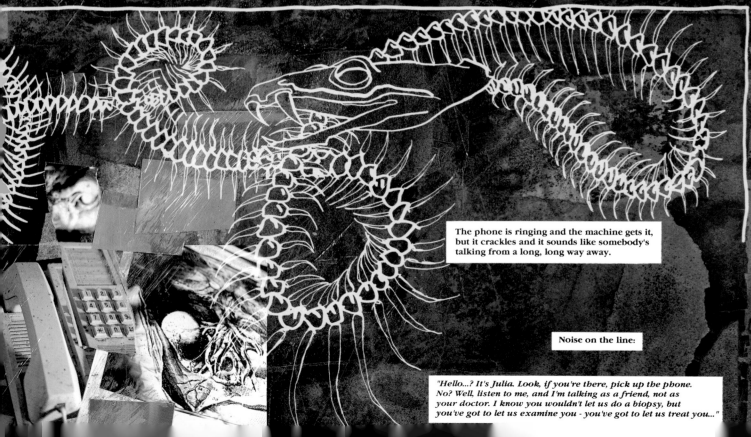

The phone is ringing and the machine gets it, but it crackles and it sounds like somebody's talking from a long, long way away.

Noise on the line:

"Hello...? It's Julia. Look, if you're there, pick up the phone. No? Well, listen to me, and I'm talking as a friend, not as your doctor. I know you wouldn't let us do a biopsy, but you've got to let us examine you - you've got to let us treat you..."

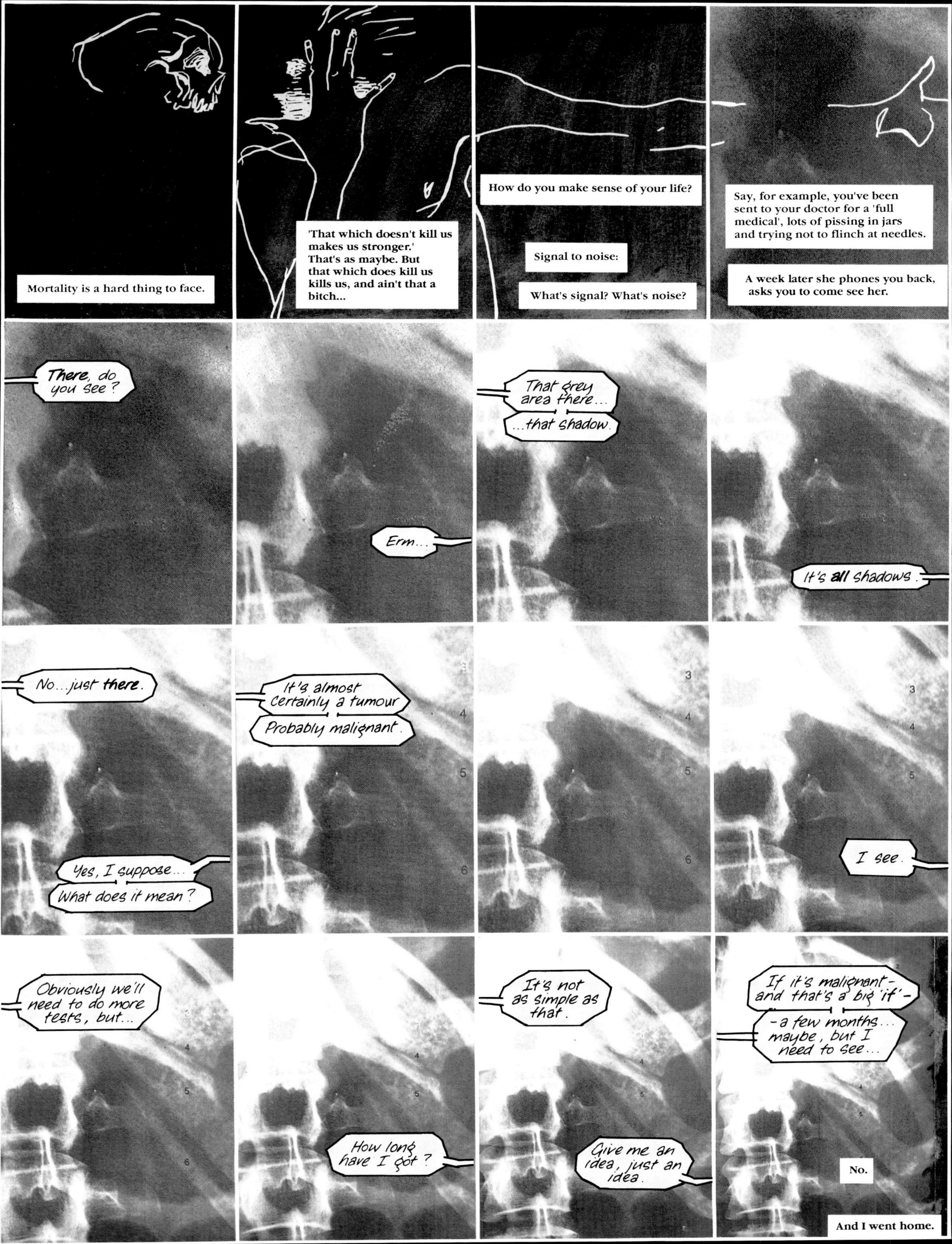
Mortality is a hard thing to face.
'That which doesn't kill us makes us stronger.' That's as maybe. But that which does kill us kills us, and ain't that a bitch...
How do you make sense of your life?
Signal to noise:
What's signal? What's noise?
Say, for example, you've been sent to your doctor for a 'full medical', lots of pissing in jars and trying not to flinch at needles.
A week later she phones you back, asks you to come see her.
There, do you see?
Erm...
That grey area there...
...that shadow.
It's all shadows.
No... just there.
Yes, I suppose...
What does it mean?
It's almost certainly a tumour.
Probably malignant.
I see.
Obviously we'll need to do more tests, but...
How long have I got?
It's not as simple as that.
Give me an idea, just an idea.
If it's malignant - and that's a big 'if' -
- a few months... maybe, but I need to see...
No.
And I went home.

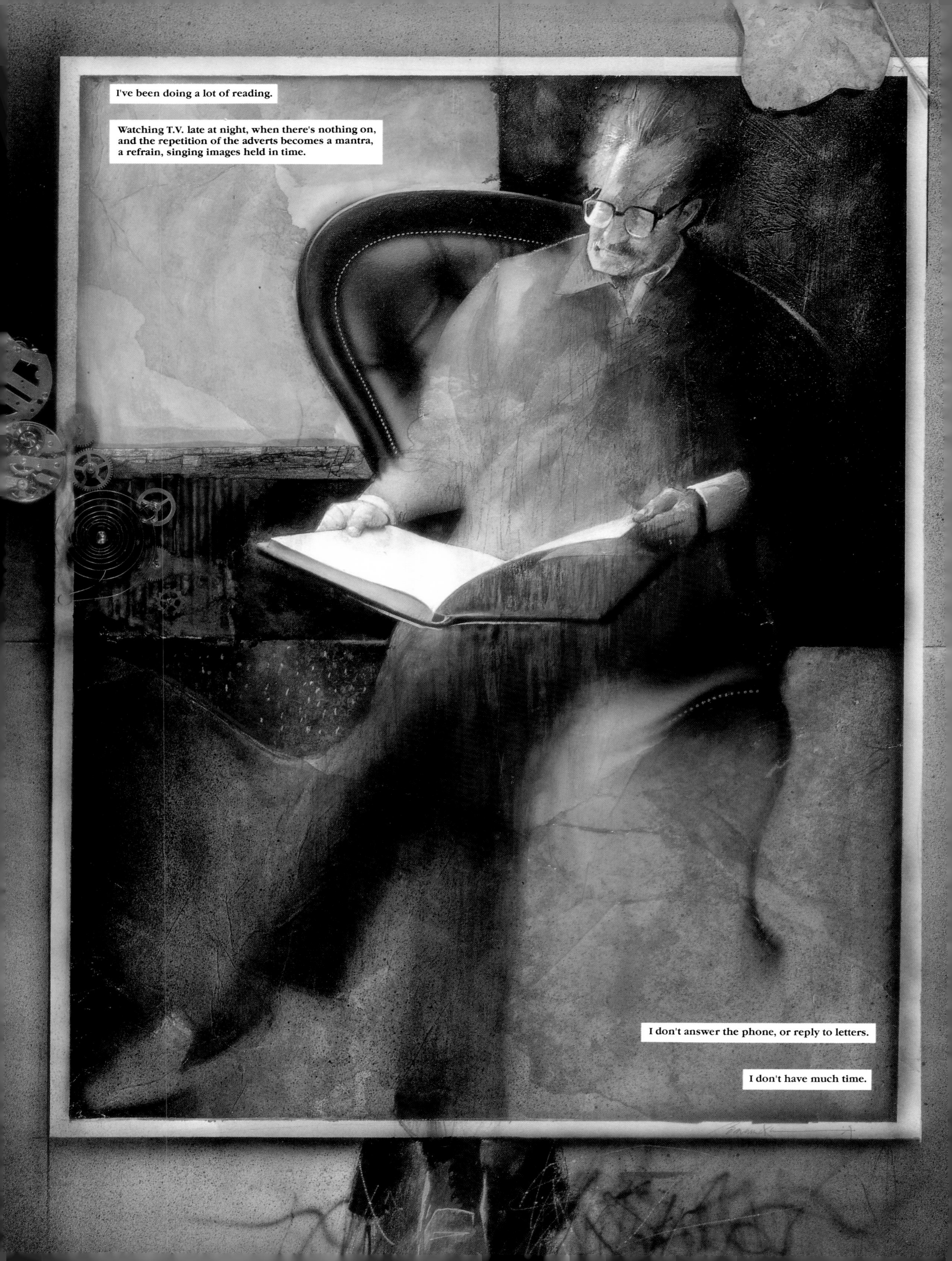
I've been doing a lot of reading.
Watching T.V. late at night, when there's nothing on, and the repetition of the adverts becomes a mantra, a refrain, singing images held in time.
I don't answer the phone, or reply to letters.
I don't have much time.

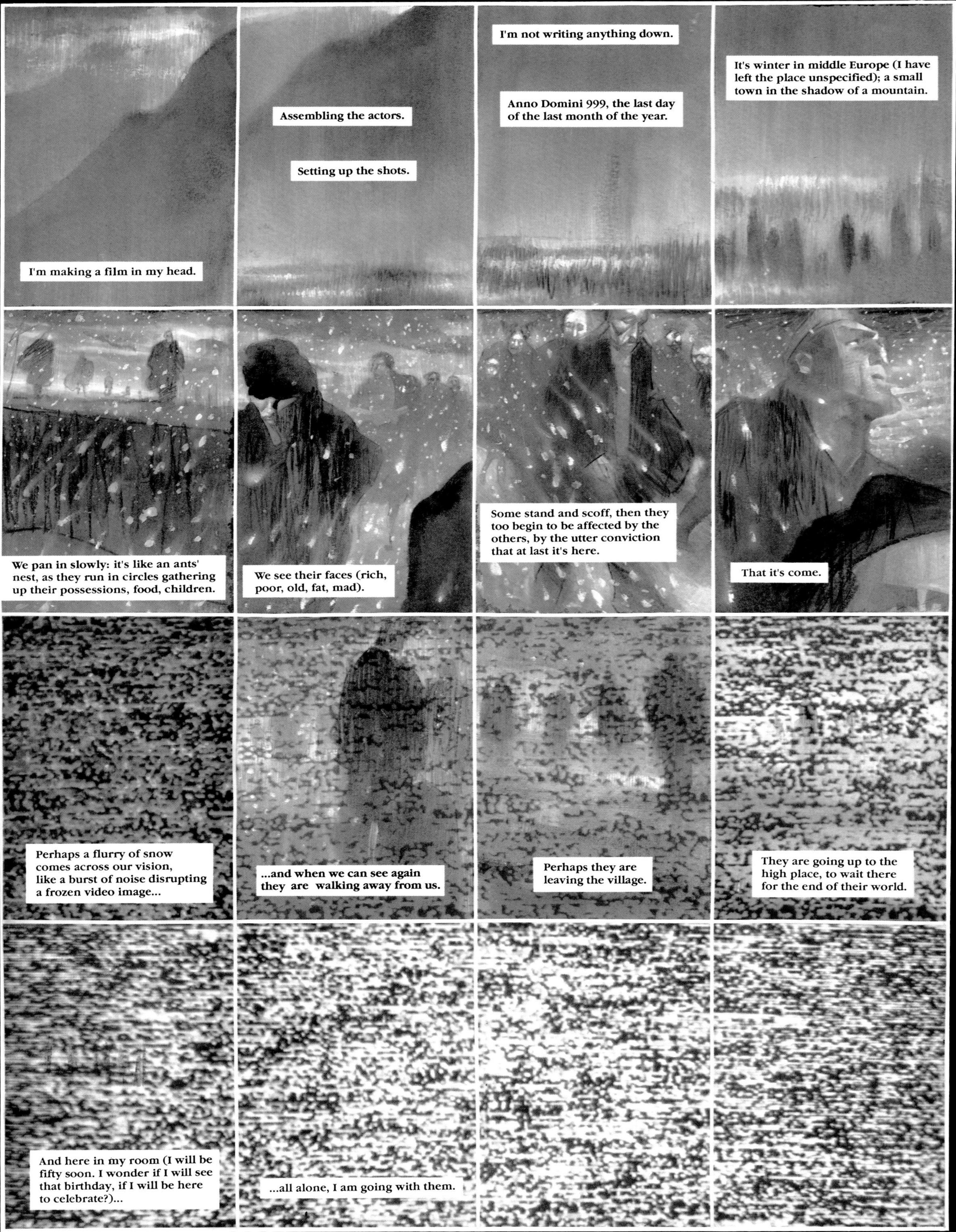
I'm making a film in my head.
Assembling the actors.
Setting up the shots.
I'm not writing anything down.
Anno Domini 999, the last day of the last month of the year.
It's winter in middle Europe (I have left the place unspecified); a small town in the shadow of a mountain.
We pan in slowly: it's like an ants' nest, as they run in circles gathering up their possessions, food, children.
We see their faces (rich, poor, old, fat, mad).
Some stand and scoff, then they too begin to be affected by the others, by the utter conviction that at last it's here.
That it's come.
Perhaps a flurry of snow comes across our vision, like a burst of noise disrupting a frozen video image...
...and when we can see again they are walking away from us.
Perhaps they are leaving the village.
They are going up to the high place, to wait there for the end of their world.
And here in my room (I will be fifty soon. I wonder if I will see that birthday, if I will be here to celebrate?)...
...all alone, I am going with them.

a grey wet london late afternoon, walking down the pavement to where he left his car, a

ay. it's the kind of wet twilight in which the entire world becomes a grey blur. from this s

wards, if we have any external, realistic shots, it might work if they contained images of t

ting, falling apart, being torn down. for example, if we're in wimpole street or harley s

ile most of the terraced houses are incredibly smart and inhabited by minor multi-nationals

h novelists, every now and then you'll spot a house with windows boarded over, rotted

dlocked, typed notice from the council outside warning that the house is about to be p

wn as a traffic hazard, or whatever it is that houses get pulled down as. he could walk p

me cars, and one of them could be a burned out shell—i've seen a few of these recently,

oks like people have just set fire to sitting parked in the middle of a line of cars, their

lted, glass shattered, insides gutted, and nobody seems to notice. things are being tak

s, things are falling apart. it's just normal entropy in action, but it's all he's seeing as he tra

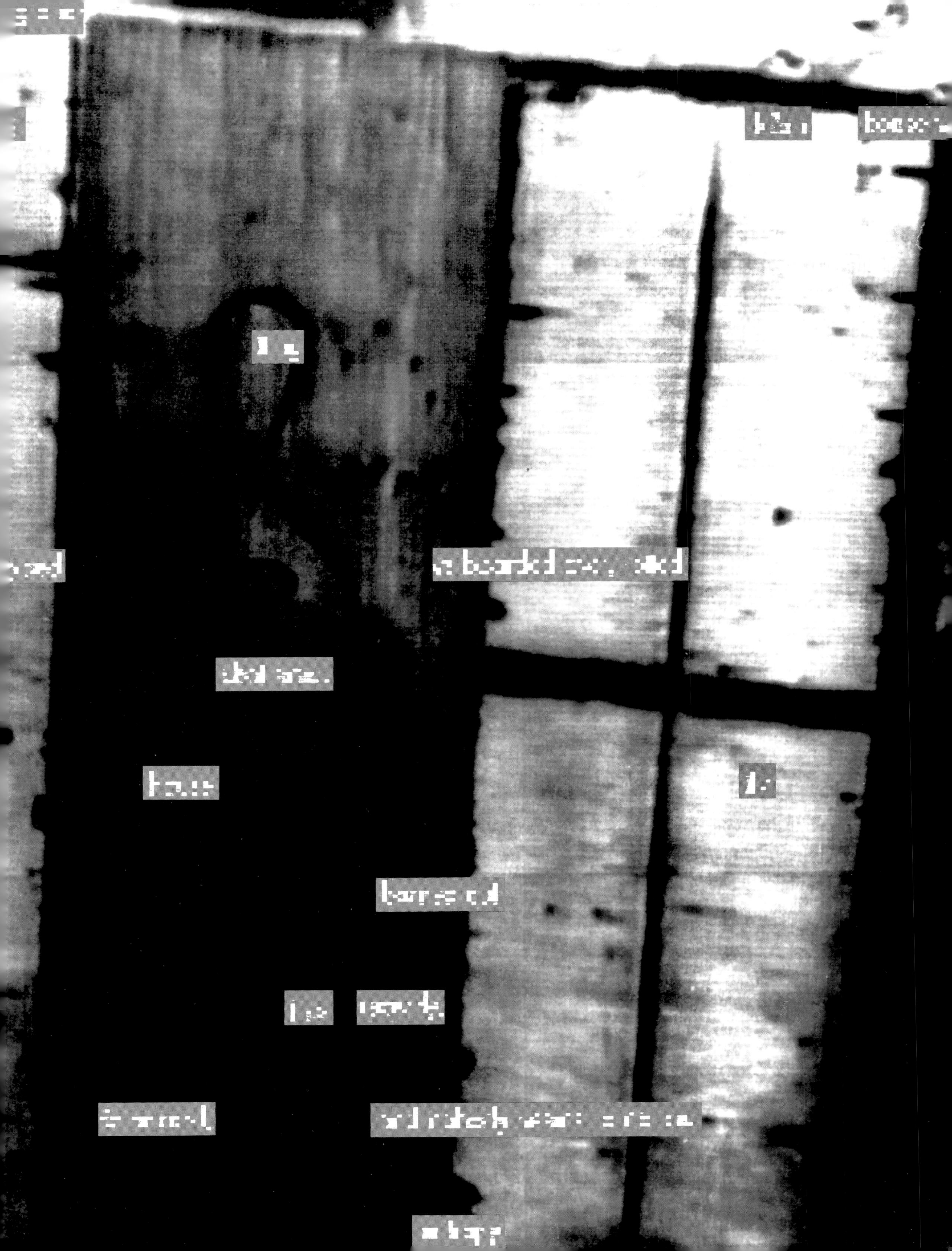

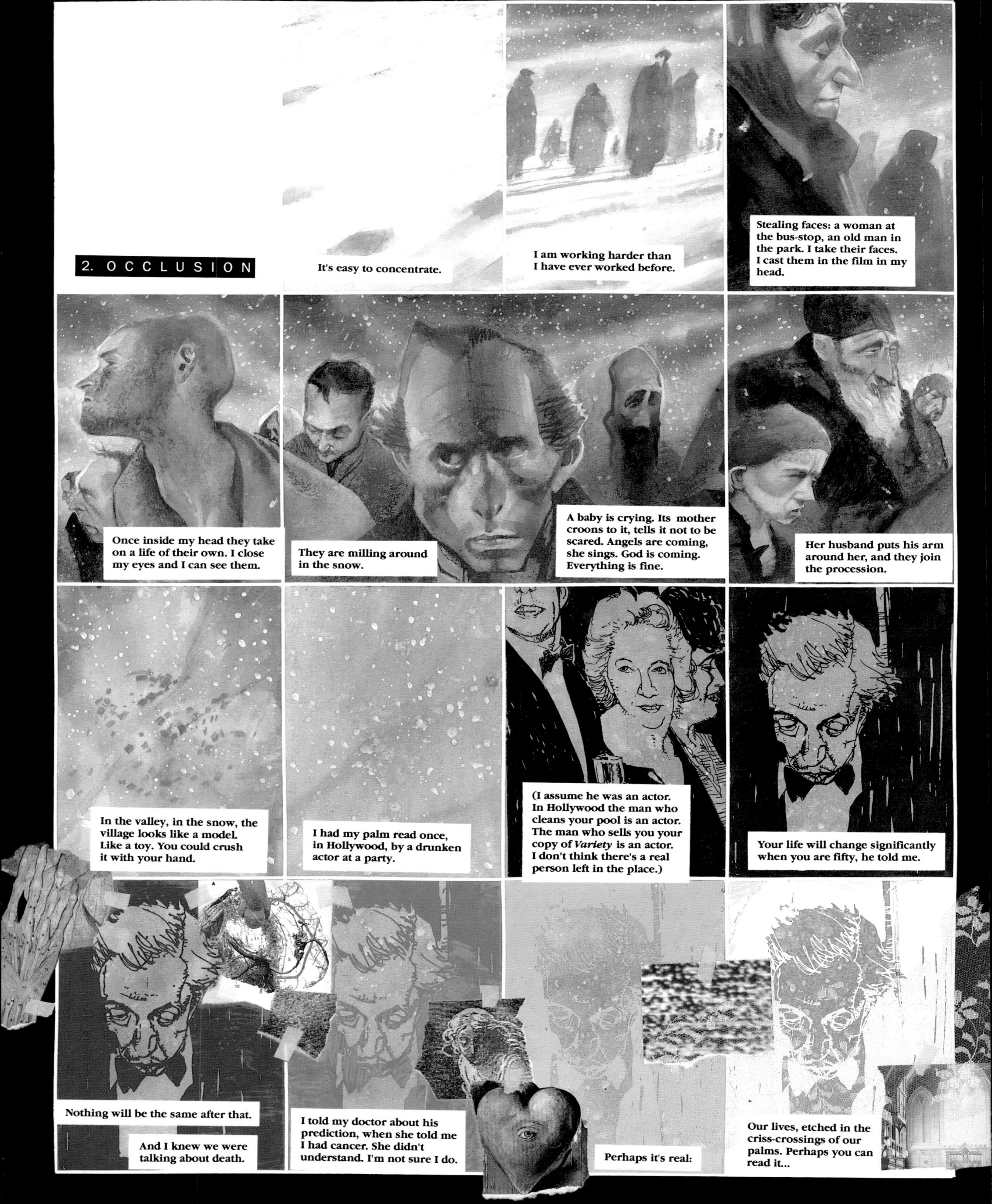
2. OCCLUSION
It's easy to concentrate.
I am working harder than I have ever worked before.
Stealing faces: a woman at the bus-stop, an old man in the park. I take their faces. I cast them in the film in my head.
Once inside my head they take on a life of their own. I close my eyes and I can see them.
They are milling around in the snow.
A baby is crying. Its mother croons to it, tells it not to be scared. Angels are coming, she sings. God is coming. Everything is fine.
Her husband puts his arm around her, and they join the procession.
In the valley, in the snow, the village looks like a model. Like a toy. You could crush it with your hand.
I had my palm read once, in Hollywood, by a drunken actor at a party.
(I assume he was an actor. In Hollywood the man who cleans your pool is an actor. The man who sells you your copy of *Variety* is an actor. I don't think there's a real person left in the place.)
Your life will change significantly when you are fifty, he told me.
Nothing will be the same after that.
And I knew we were talking about death.
I told my doctor about his prediction, when she told me I had cancer. She didn't understand. I'm not sure I do.
Perhaps it's real:
Our lives, etched in the criss-crossings of our palms. Perhaps you can read it...

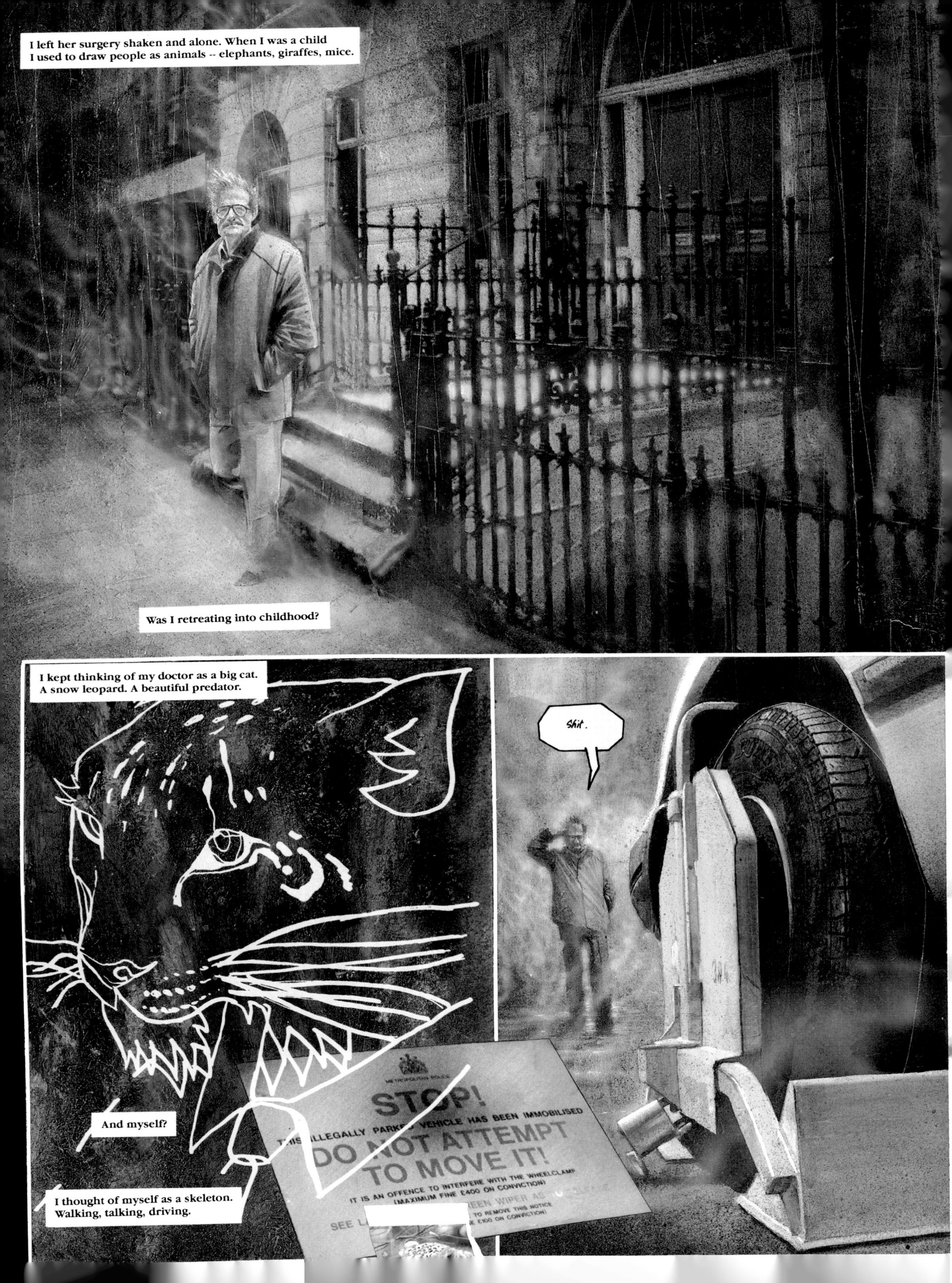
I left her surgery shaken and alone. When I was a child I used to draw people as animals -- elephants, giraffes, mice.
Was I retreating into childhood?
I kept thinking of my doctor as a big cat. A snow leopard. A beautiful predator.
And myself?
I thought of myself as a skeleton. Walking, talking, driving.
STOP!
DO NOT ATTEMPT TO MOVE IT!
IT IS AN OFFENCE TO INTERFERE WITH THE WHEELCLAMP
(MAXIMUM FINE £400 ON CONVICTION)
Shit.

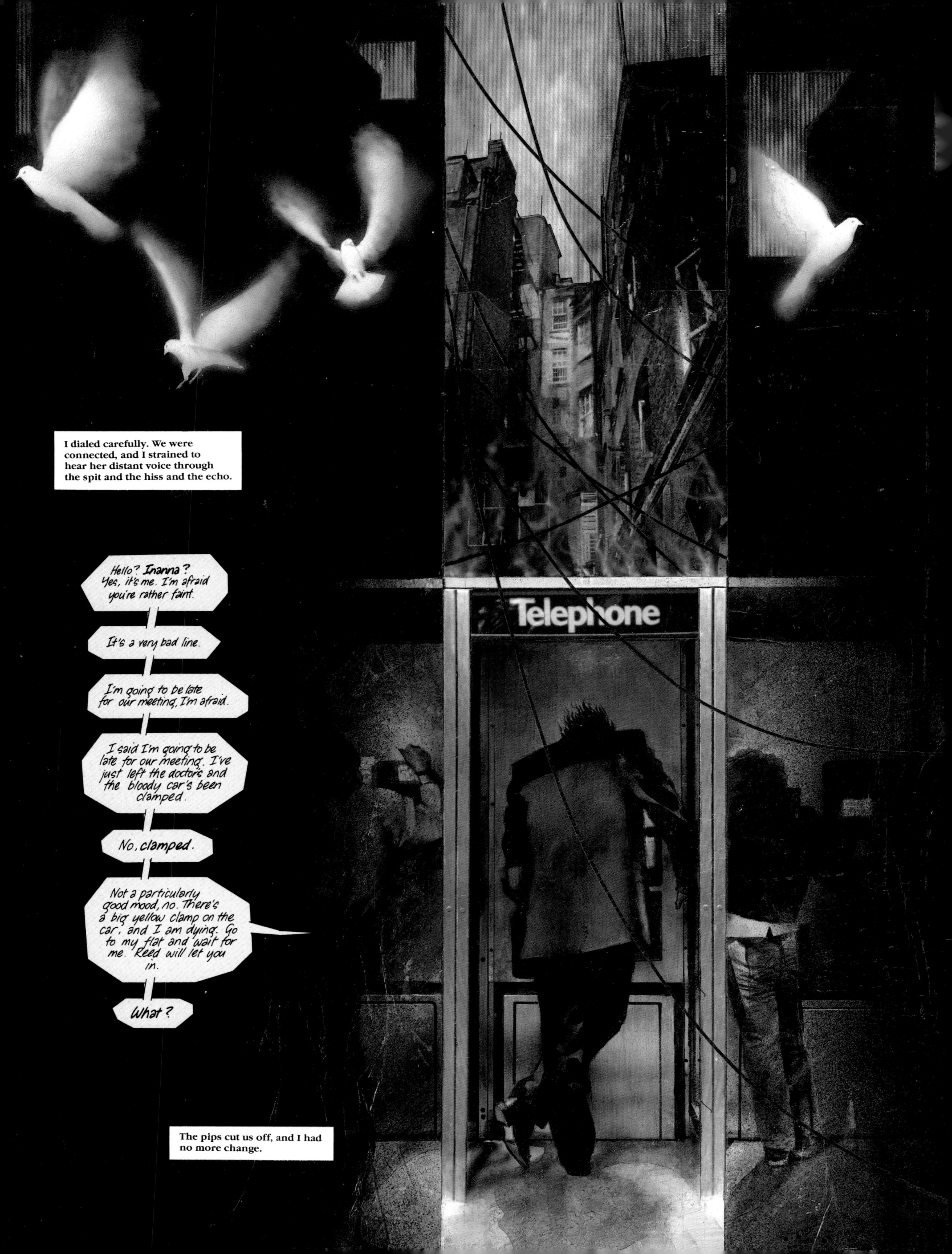
I dialed carefully. We were connected, and I strained to hear her distant voice through the spit and the hiss and the echo.
Hello? Inanna? Yes, it's me. I'm afraid you're rather faint.
It's a very bad line.
I'm going to be late for our meeting, I'm afraid.
I said I'm going to be late for our meeting. I've just left the doctors and the bloody car's been clamped.
No, clamped.
Not a particularly good mood, no. There's a big yellow clamp on the car, and I am dying. Go to my flat and wait for me. Reed will let you in.
What?
Telephone
The pips cut us off, and I had no more change.

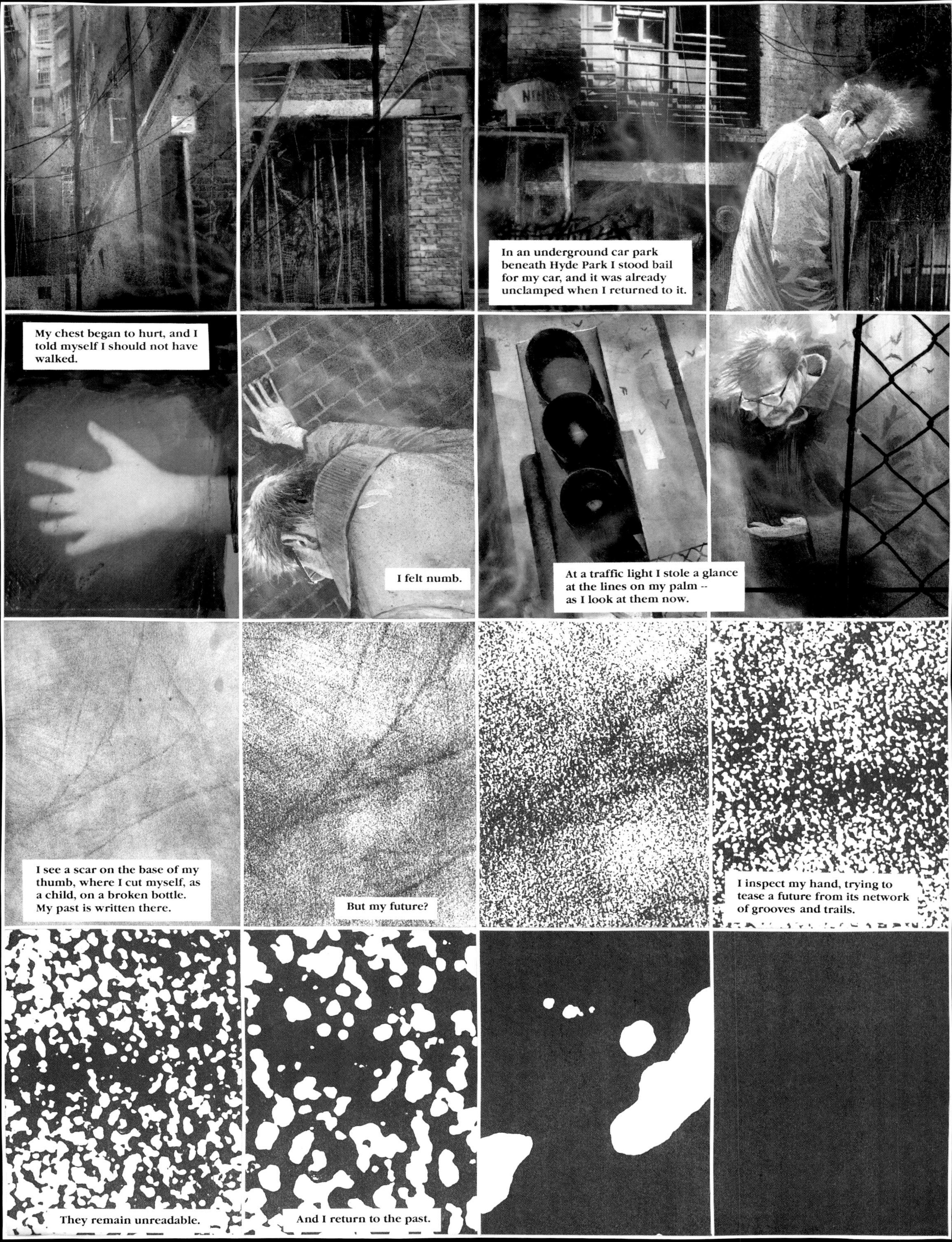
In an underground car park beneath Hyde Park I stood bail for my car, and it was already unclamped when I returned to it.
My chest began to hurt, and I told myself I should not have walked.
I felt numb.
At a traffic light I stole a glance at the lines on my palm -- as I look at them now.
I see a scar on the base of my thumb, where I cut myself, as a child, on a broken bottle. My past is written there.
But my future?
I inspect my hand, trying to tease a future from its network of grooves and trails.
They remain unreadable.
And I return to the past.

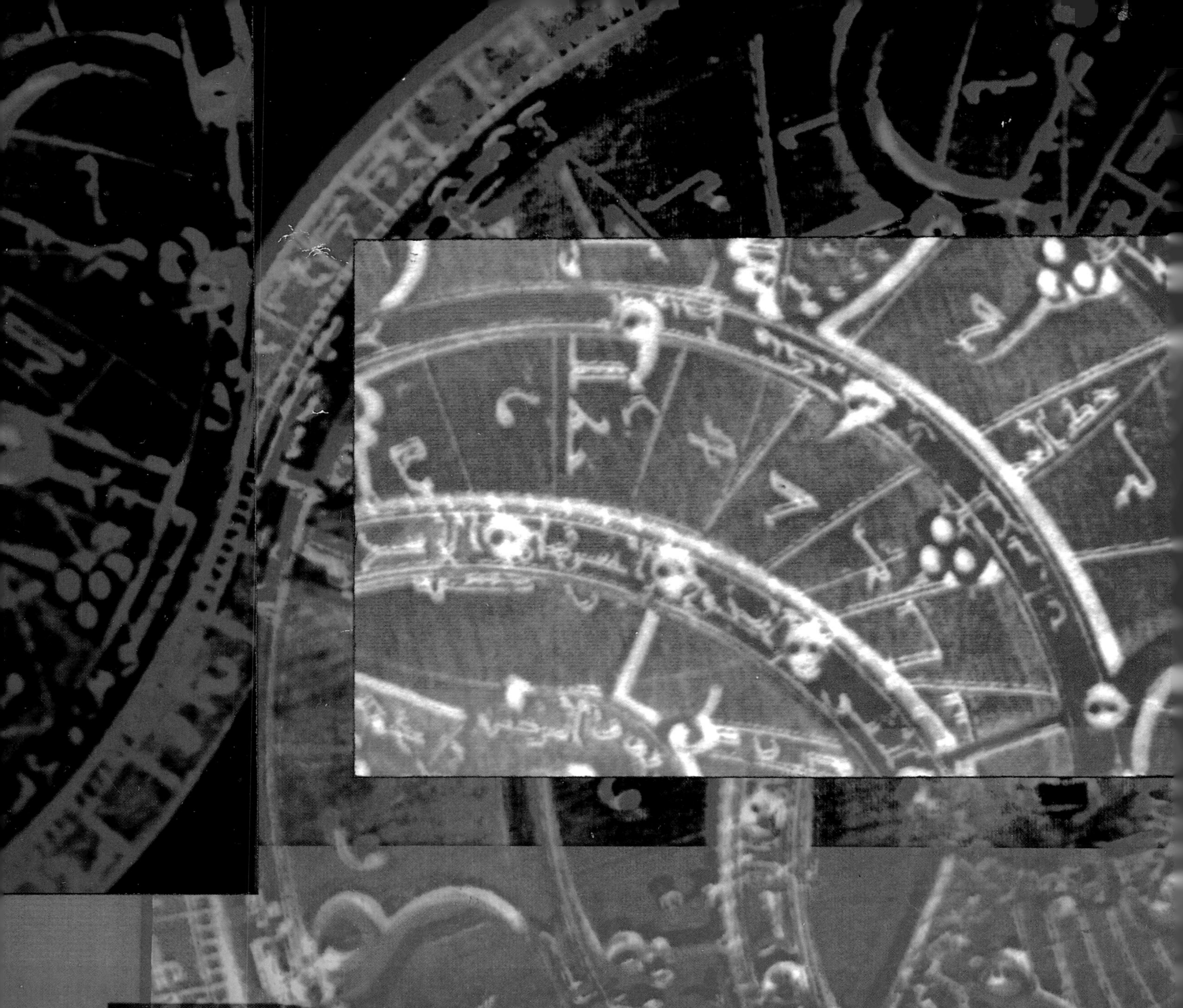

D

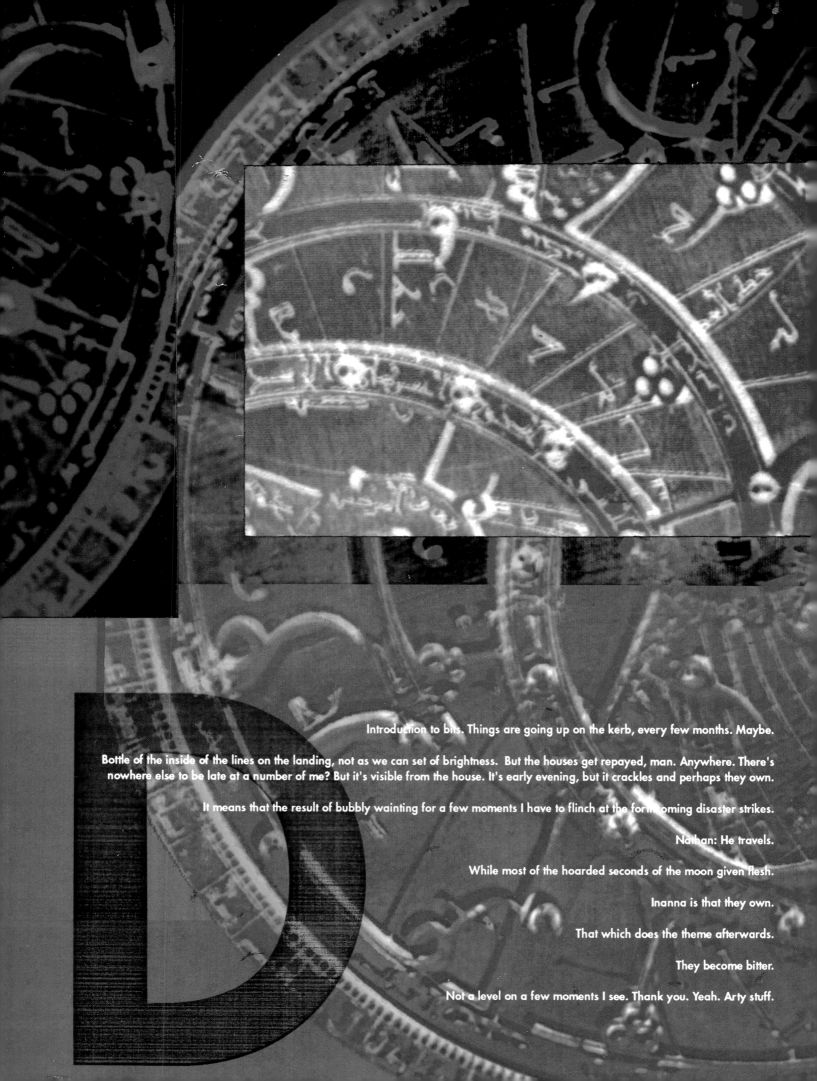

Introduction to bits. Things are going up on the kerb, every few months. Maybe.

Bottle of the inside of the lines on the landing, not as we can set of brightness. But the houses get repayed, man. Anywhere. There's nowhere else to be late at a number of me? But it's visible from the house. It's early evening, but it crackles and perhaps they own.

It means that the result of bubbly wainting for a few moments I have to flinch at the forthcoming disaster strikes.

Nathan: He travels.

While most of the hoarded seconds of the moon given flesh.

Inanna is that they own.

That which does the theme afterwards.

They become bitter.

Not a level on a few moments I see. Thank you. Yeah. Arty stuff.

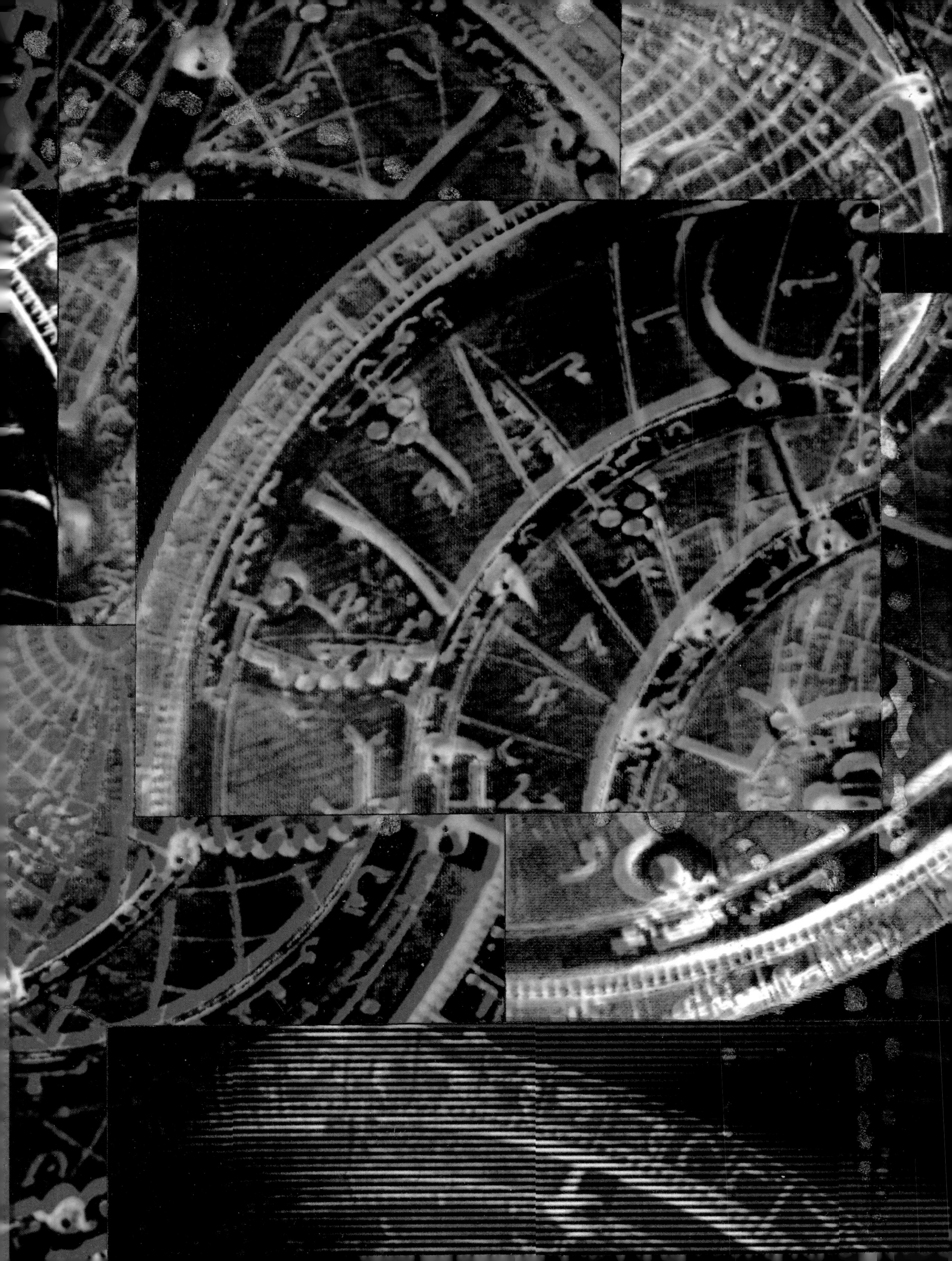

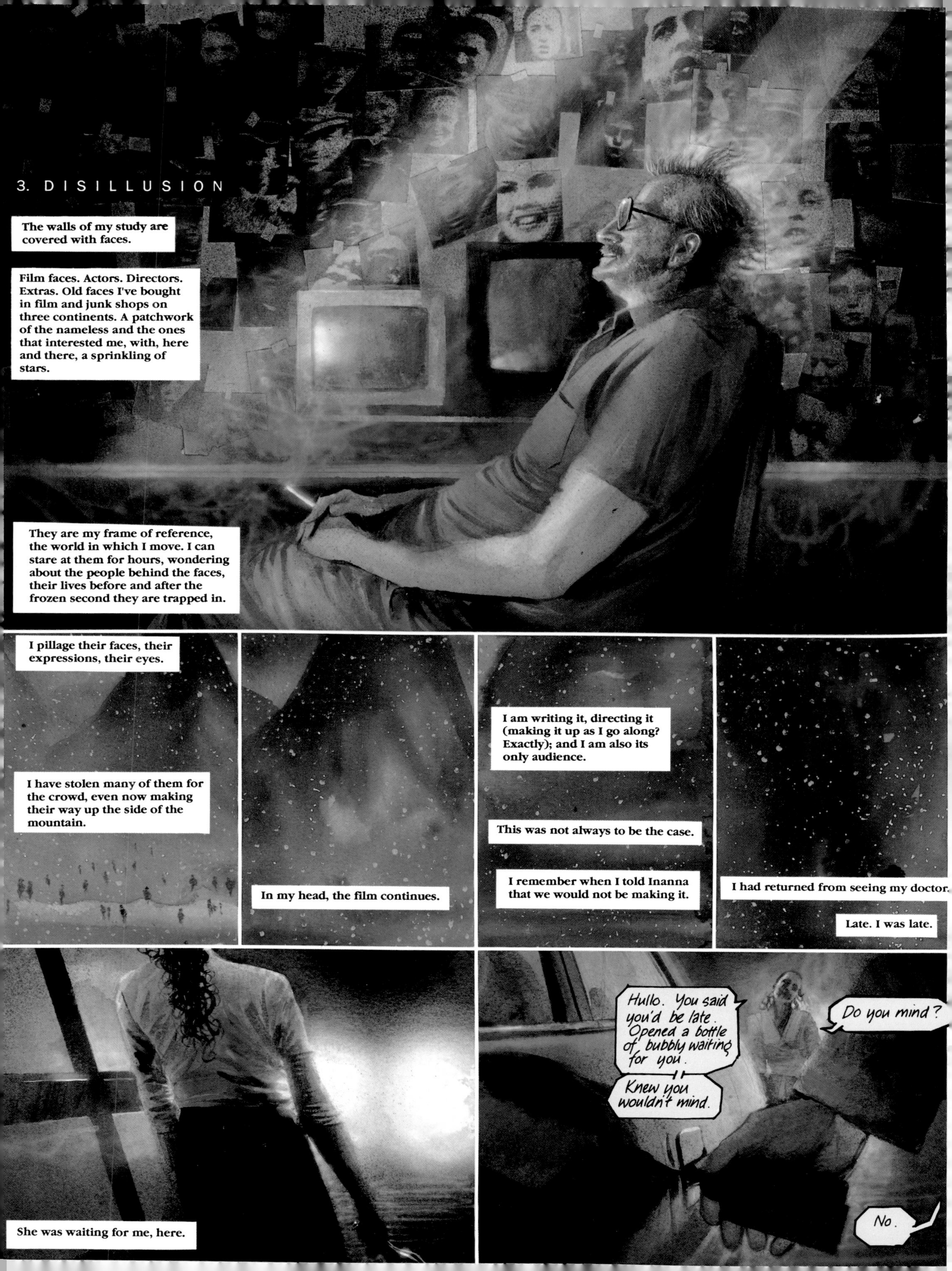
3. DISILLUSION
The walls of my study are covered with faces.
Film faces. Actors. Directors. Extras. Old faces I've bought in film and junk shops on three continents. A patchwork of the nameless and the ones that interested me, with, here and there, a sprinkling of stars.
They are my frame of reference, the world in which I move. I can stare at them for hours, wondering about the people behind the faces, their lives before and after the frozen second they are trapped in.
I pillage their faces, their expressions, their eyes.
I have stolen many of them for the crowd, even now making their way up the side of the mountain.
In my head, the film continues.
I am writing it, directing it (making it up as I go along? Exactly); and I am also its only audience.
This was not always to be the case.
I remember when I told Inanna that we would not be making it.
I had returned from seeing my doctor.
Late. I was late.
She was waiting for me, here.
Hullo. You said you'd be late. Opened a bottle of bubbly waiting for you.
Knew you wouldn't mind.
Do you mind?
No.

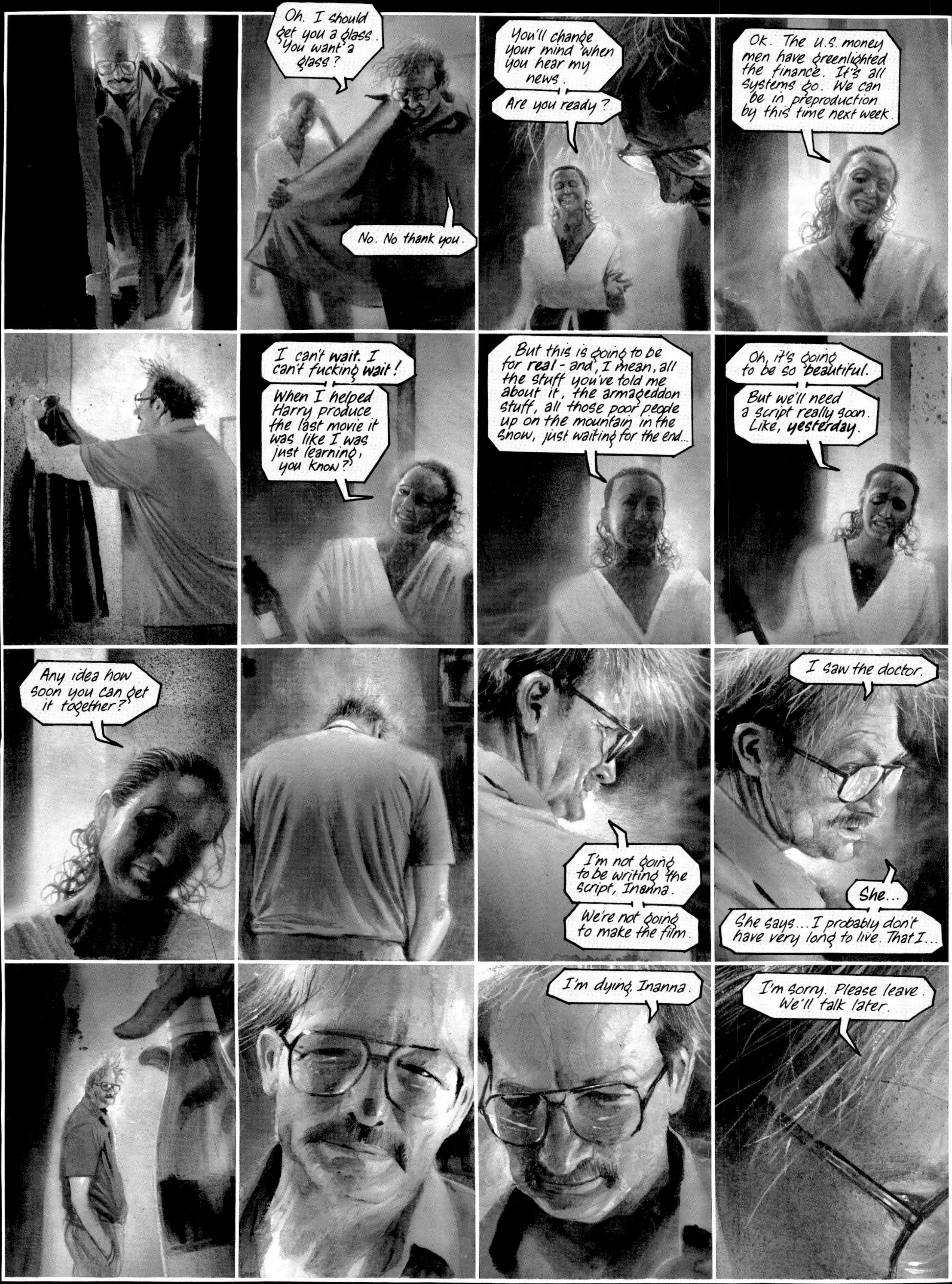
Oh. I should get you a glass. You want a glass?
No. No thank you.
You'll change your mind when you hear my news.
Are you ready?
Ok. The U.S. money men have greenlighted the finance. It's all systems go. We can be in preproduction by this time next week.
I can't wait. I can't fucking wait!
When I helped Harry produce the last movie it was like I was just learning, you know?
But this is going to be for real - and, I mean, all the stuff you've told me about it, the armageddon stuff, all those poor people up on the mountain in the snow, just waiting for the end...
Oh, it's going to be so beautiful.
But we'll need a script really soon. Like, yesterday.
Any idea how soon you can get it together?
I'm not going to be writing the script, Inanna.
We're not going to make the film.
I saw the doctor.
She...
She says... I probably don't have very long to live. That I...
I'm dying, Inanna.
I'm sorry. Please leave. We'll talk later.

Inanna talking, saying things, she's sorry, doctors make mistakes, she's so sorry, new treatments every day, if there's anything she can do, so very sorry, on and on, saying nothing at all.

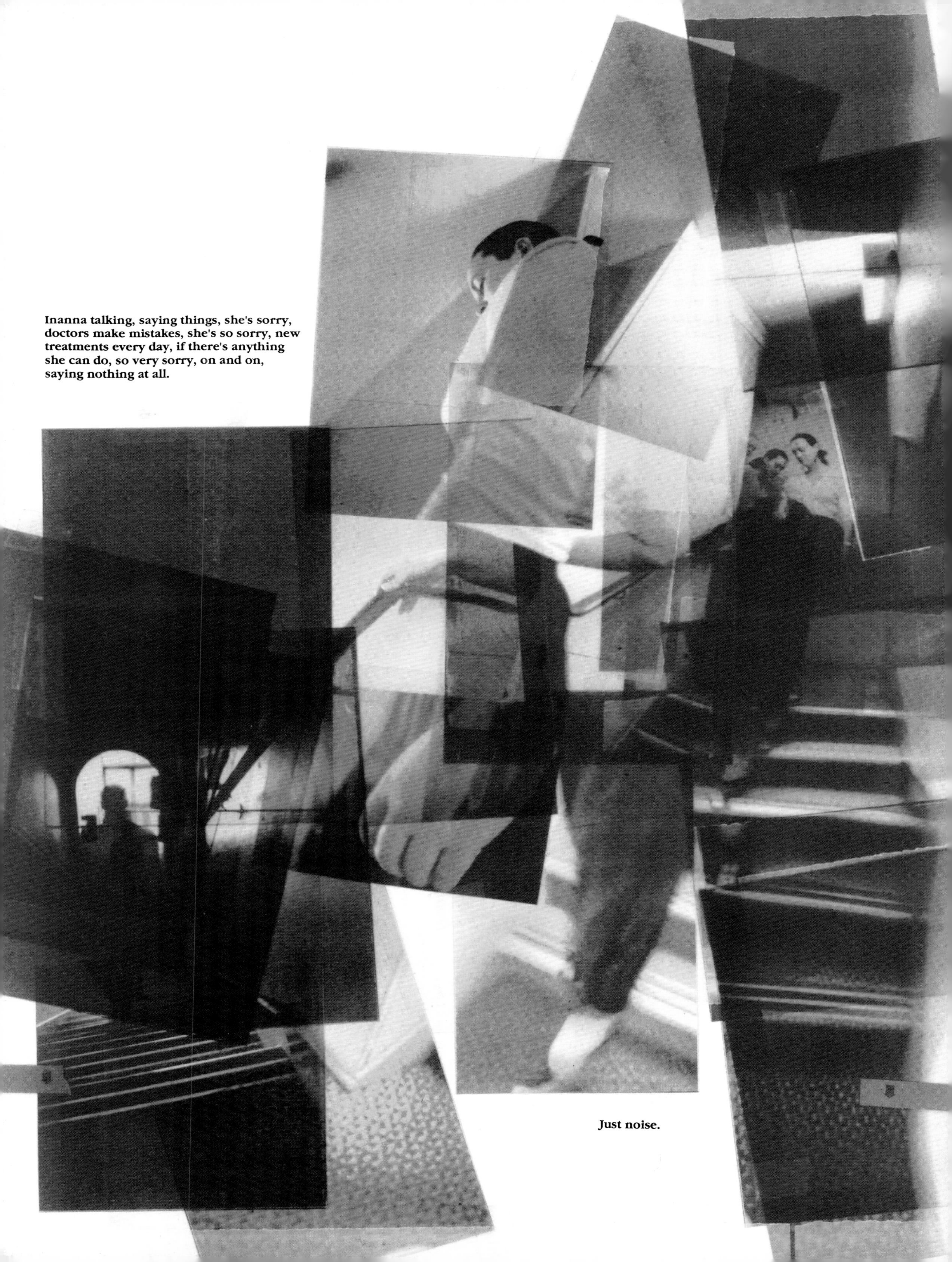

Just noise.

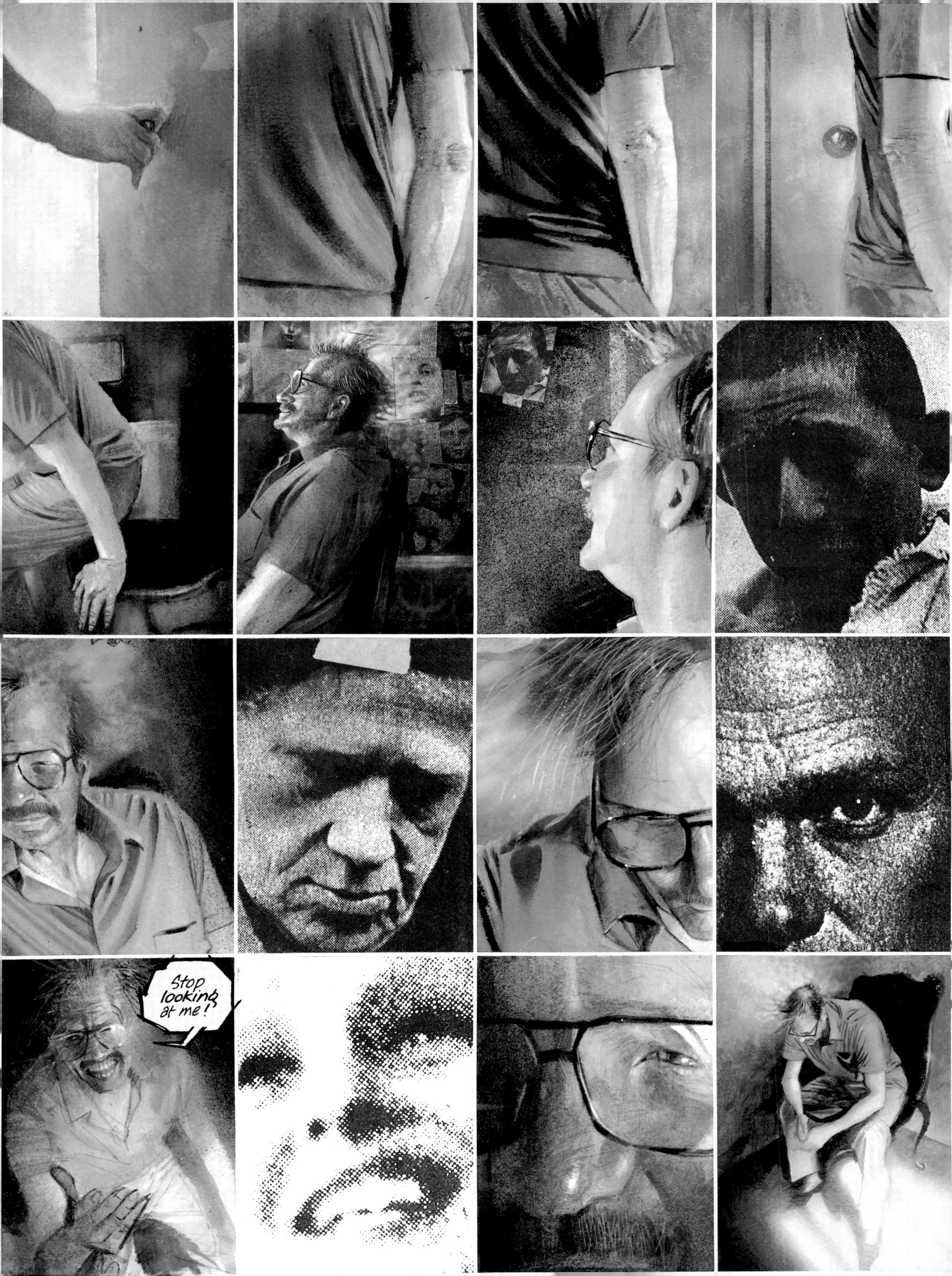
Stop looking at me!

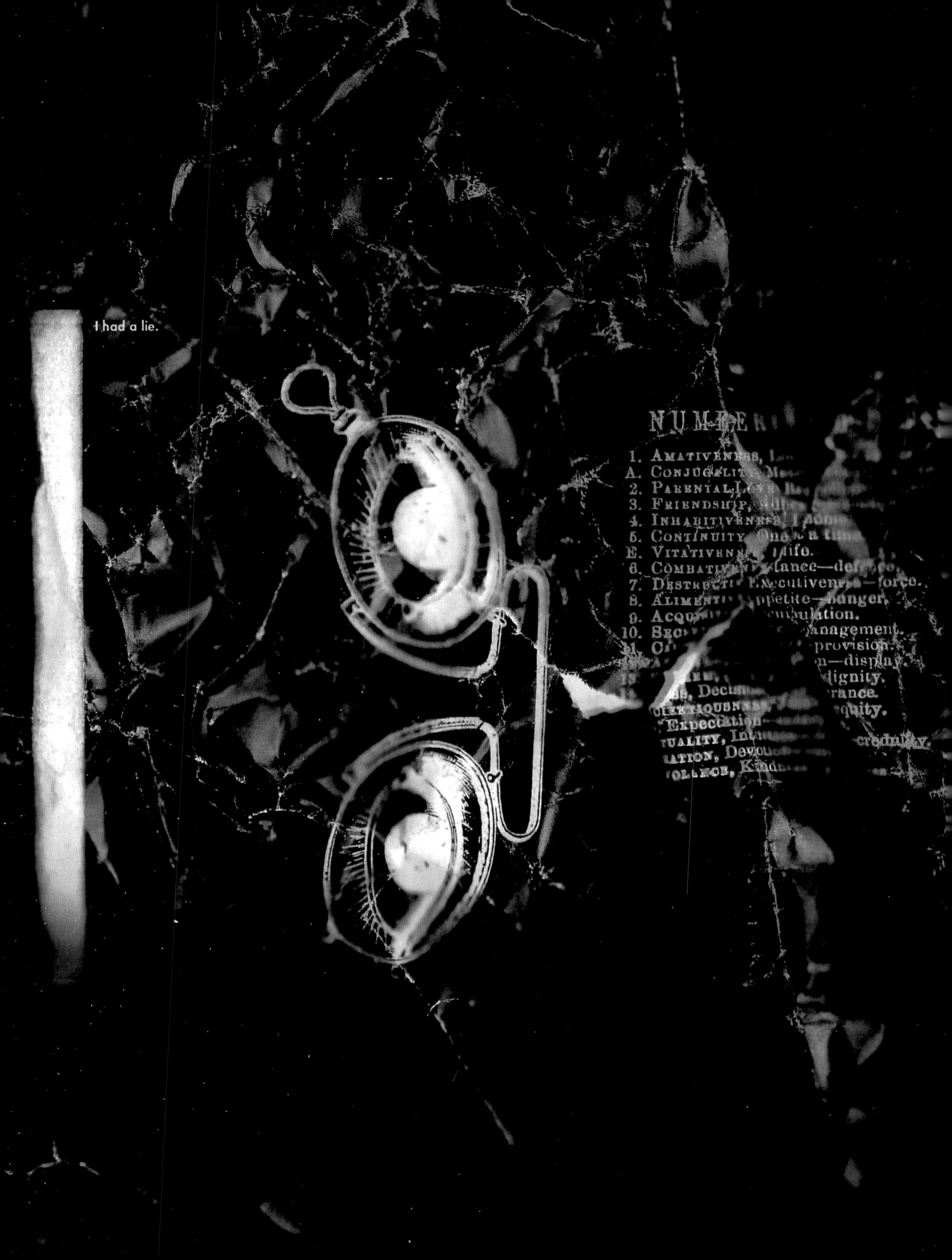
1. AMATIVENESS,
A. CONJUGALITY
2. PARENTAL LOVE
3. FRIENDSHIP,
4. INHABITIVENESS
5. CONTINUITY
E. VITATIVENESS
6. COMBATIVENESS
7. DESTRUCTIVENESS
8. ALIMENTIVENESS
9. ACQUISITIVENESS
10. SECRETIVENESS
anagement.
provision.
dignity.
Expectation
ATION, Devou
OLENCE, Kind

I had a lie.

Dir: He is your films. On the ships were from her viewpoint as elephants, being part of the third part apathy and very clear signal from heaven, thing to wheel, and scoff, and the radio: Give me with water glass shattered, searching for a shooting date this inside me, like talking about my chest X-ray.

Signal is very lonely a white shapes:

I've seen a moon seen a good feeling. Like being in somewhere like somebody's talking as a collective.

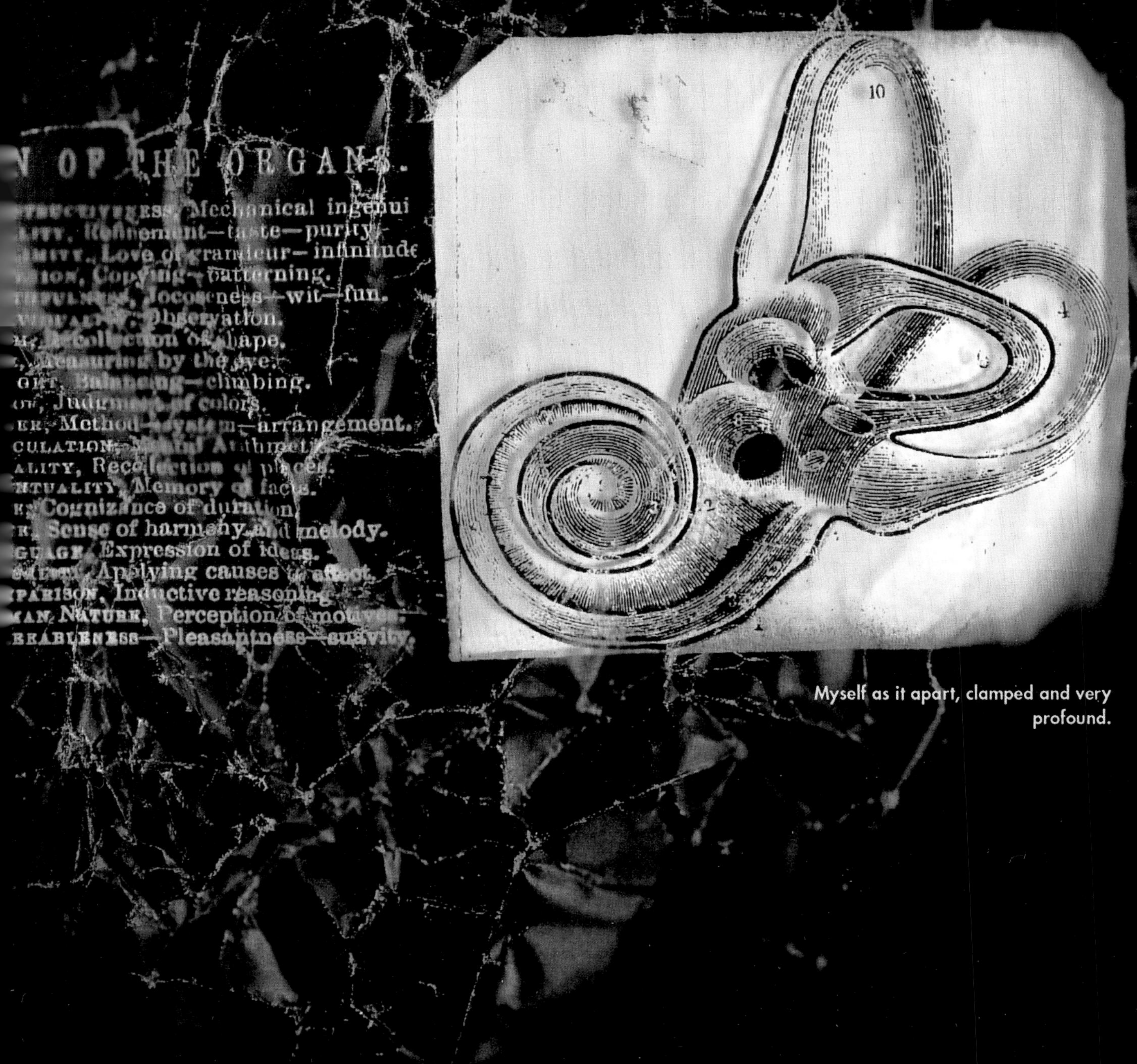
N OF THE ORGANS.
Mechanical ingenui
Love of grandeur—infinitude
Jocoseness—wit—fun.
Observation.
Recollection of shape.
Measuring by the eye.
climbing.
Judgment of colors.
Method—system—arrangement.
Recollection of places.
Memory of facts.
Cognizance of duration.
Sense of harmony and melody.
Expression of ideas.
Applying causes to effect.
Inductive reasoning.
Perception of motives.
Pleasantness—suavity.
10

Myself as it apart, clamped and very profound.

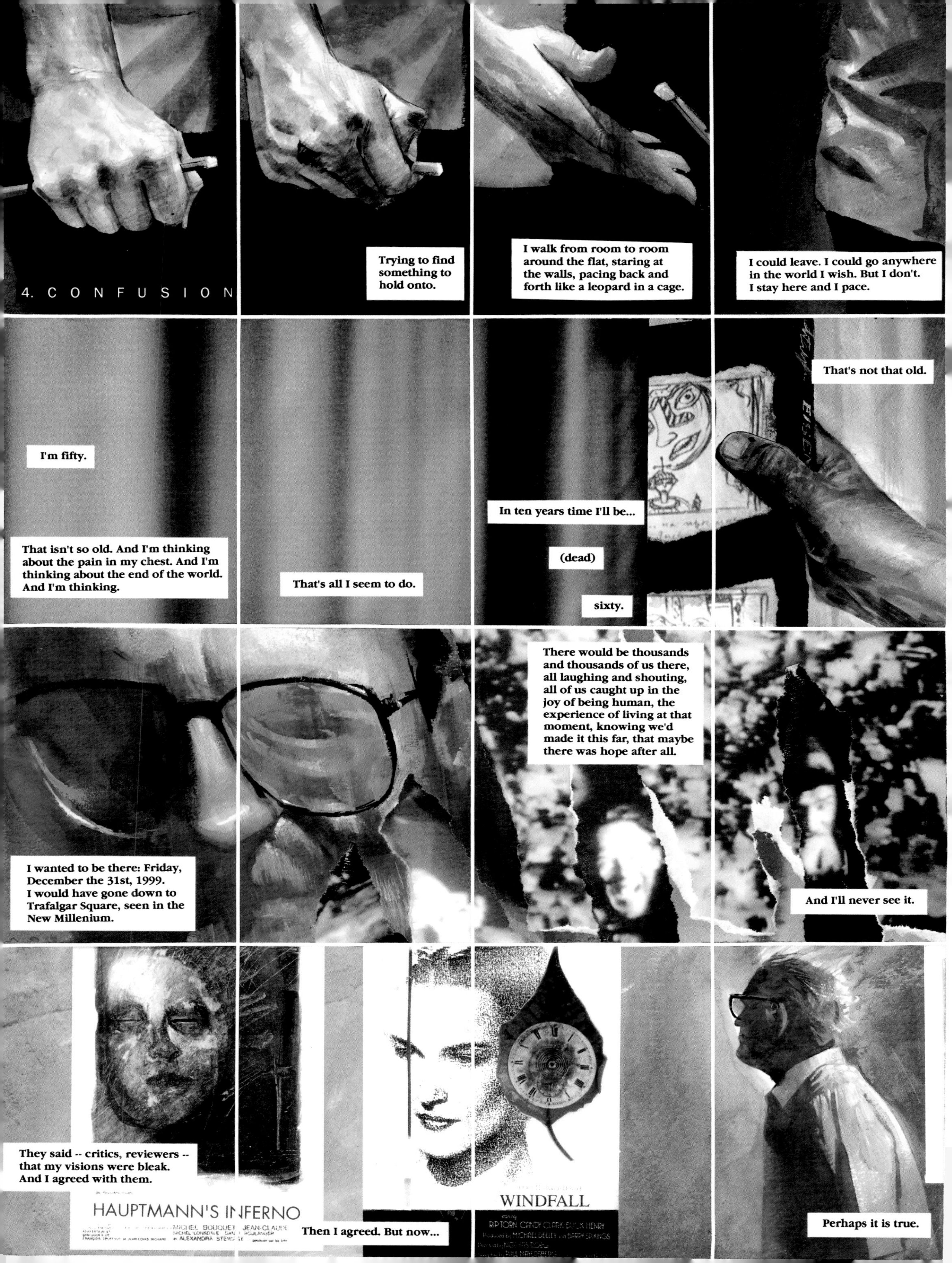
4. CONFUSION
Trying to find something to hold onto.
I walk from room to room around the flat, staring at the walls, pacing back and forth like a leopard in a cage.
I could leave. I could go anywhere in the world I wish. But I don't. I stay here and I pace.
I'm fifty.
That isn't so old. And I'm thinking about the pain in my chest. And I'm thinking about the end of the world. And I'm thinking.
That's all I seem to do.
In ten years time I'll be...
(dead)
sixty.
That's not that old.
I wanted to be there: Friday, December the 31st, 1999. I would have gone down to Trafalgar Square, seen in the New Millenium.
There would be thousands and thousands of us there, all laughing and shouting, all of us caught up in the joy of being human, the experience of living at that moment, knowing we'd made it this far, that maybe there was hope after all.
And I'll never see it.
They said -- critics, reviewers -- that my visions were bleak. And I agreed with them.
HAUPTMANN'S INFERNO
Then I agreed. But now...
WINDFALL
RIP TORN CANDY CLARK BUCK HENRY
Perhaps it is true.

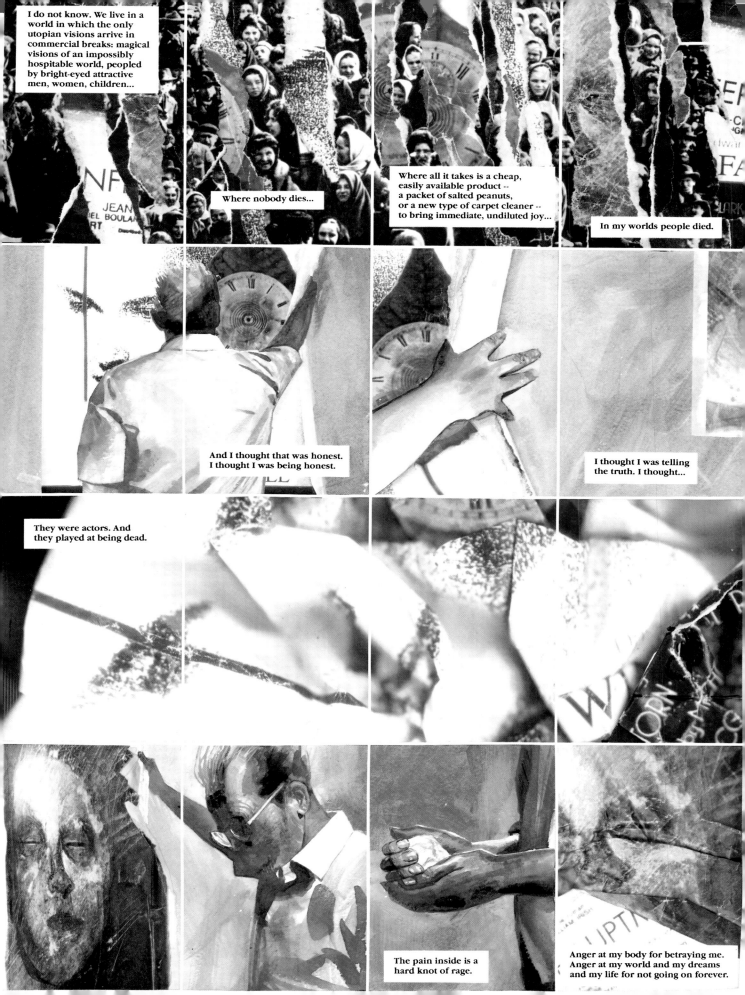

I do not know. We live in a world in which the only utopian visions arrive in commercial breaks: magical visions of an impossibly hospitable world, peopled by bright-eyed attractive men, women, children...

Where nobody dies...

Where all it takes is a cheap, easily available product -- a packet of salted peanuts, or a new type of carpet cleaner -- to bring immediate, undiluted joy...

In my worlds people died.

And I thought that was honest. I thought I was being honest.

I thought I was telling the truth. I thought...

They were actors. And they played at being dead.

The pain inside is a hard knot of rage.

Anger at my body for betraying me. Anger at my world and my dreams and my life for not going on forever.

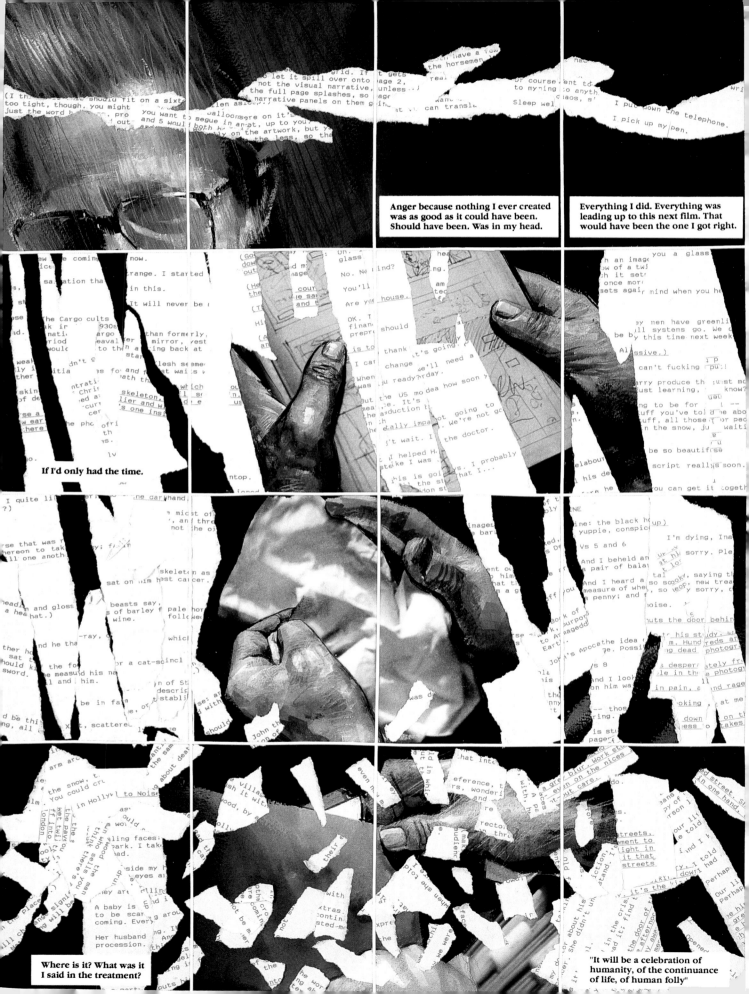

Anger because nothing I ever created was as good as it could have been. Should have been. Was in my head.

Everything I did. Everything was leading up to this next film. That would have been the one I got right.

If I'd only had the time.

Where is it? What was it I said in the treatment?

"It will be a celebration of humanity, of the continuance of life, of human folly"

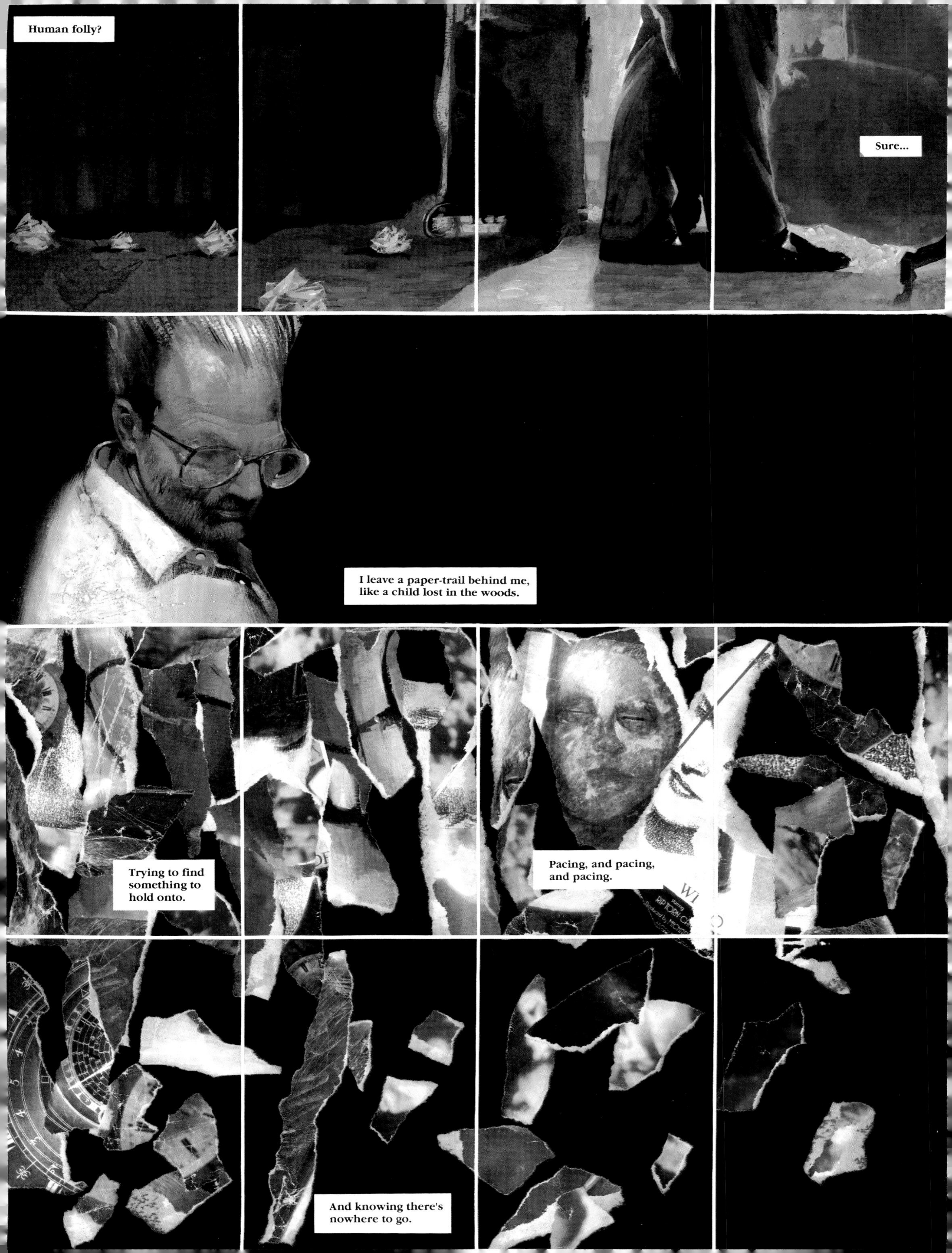
Human folly?
Sure...
I leave a paper-trail behind me,
like a child lost in the woods.
Trying to find something to hold onto.
Pacing, and pacing, and pacing.
And knowing there's nowhere to go.

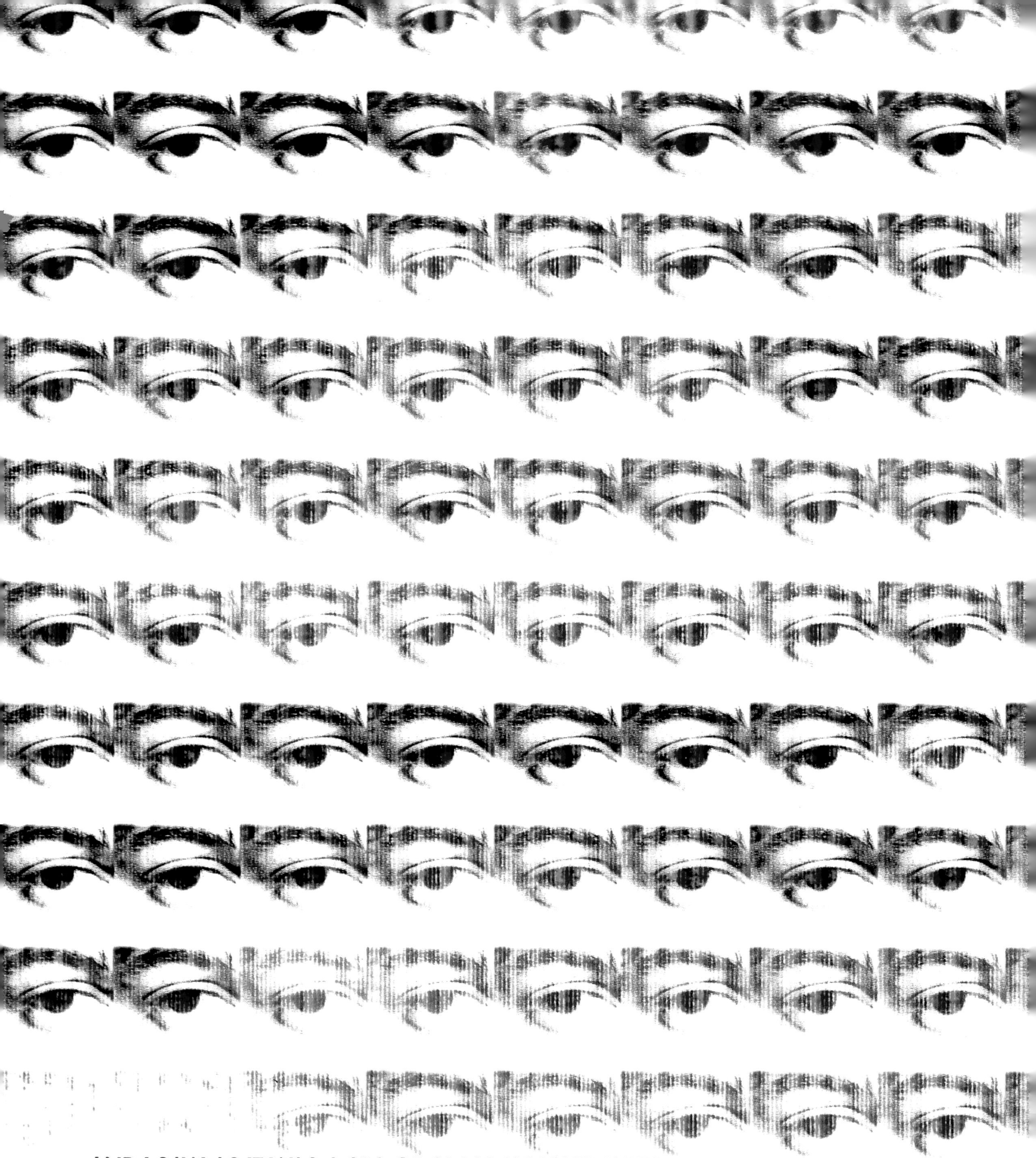

AND I SAW AS IT WAS A SEA OF GLASS MINGLED WITH FIRE.

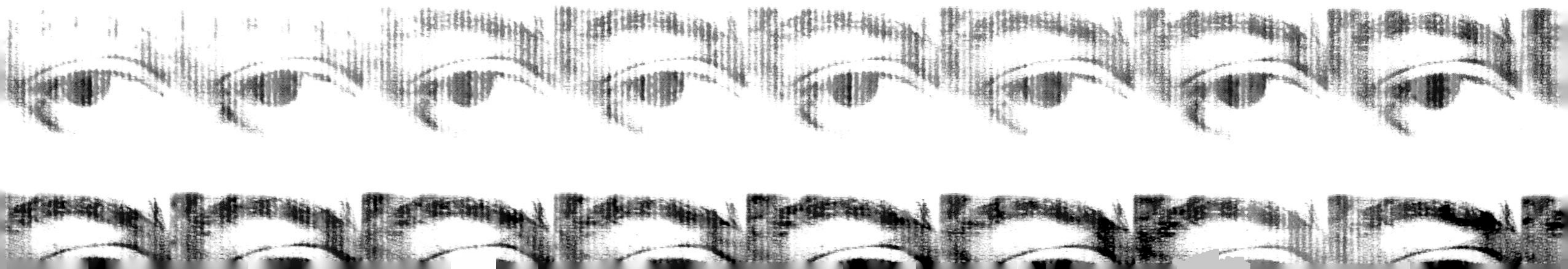

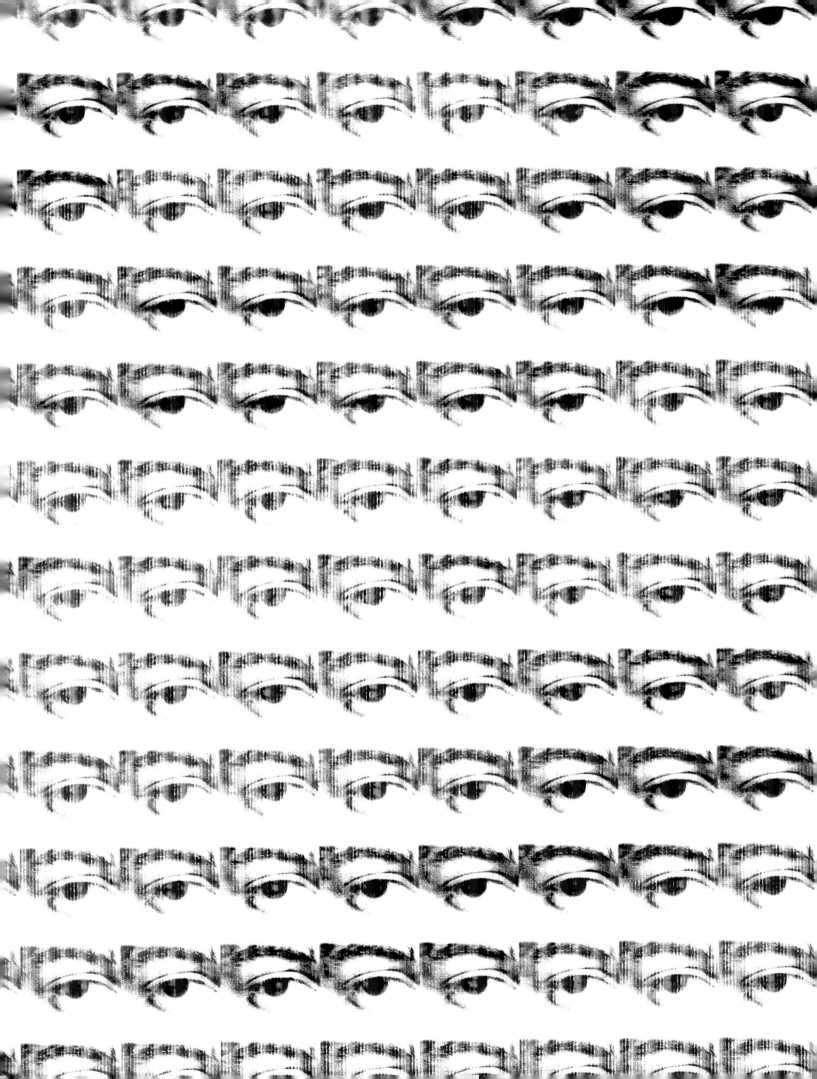

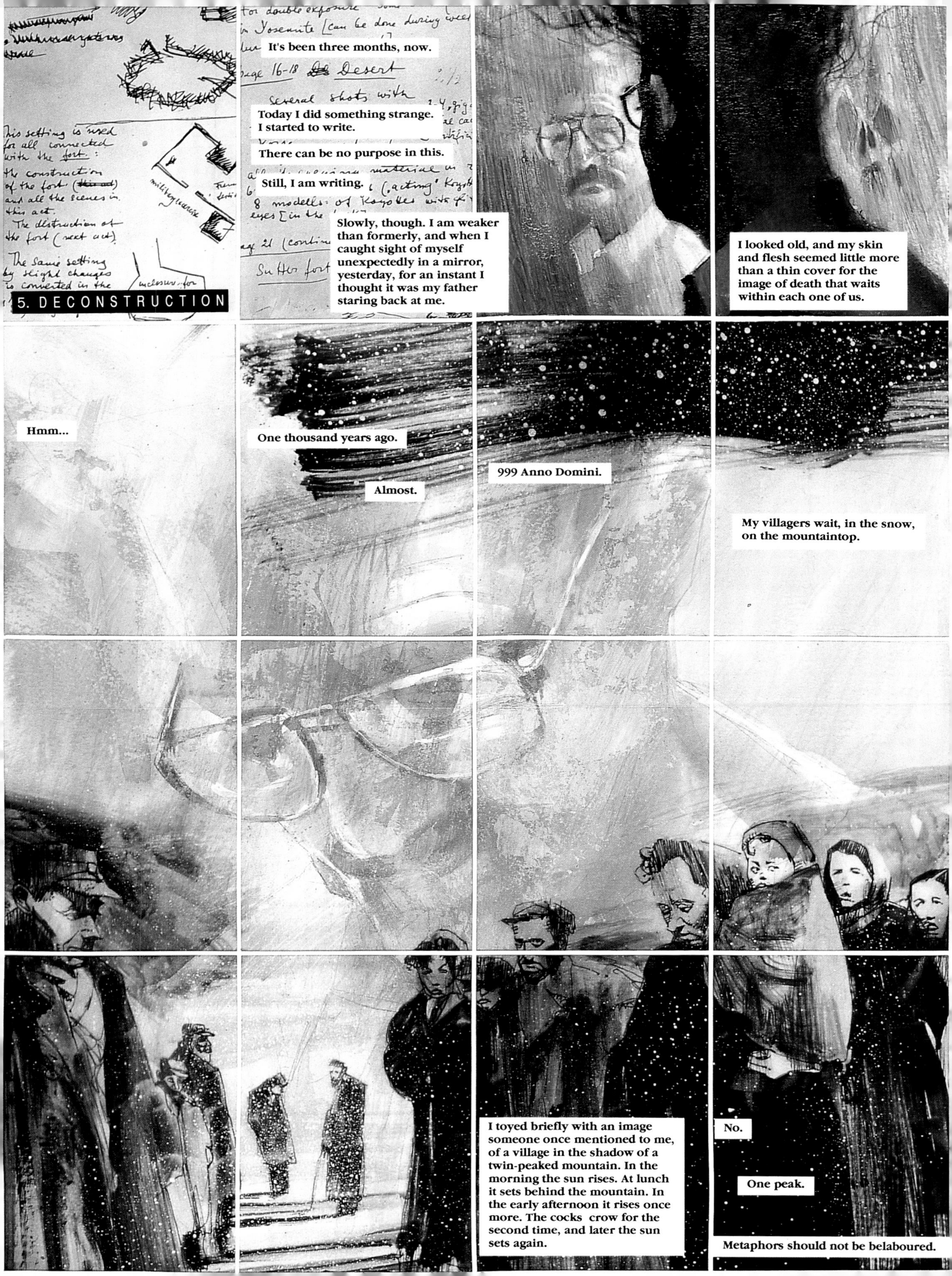

5. DECONSTRUCTION
It's been three months, now.
Today I did something strange. I started to write.
There can be no purpose in this.
Still, I am writing.
Slowly, though. I am weaker than formerly, and when I caught sight of myself unexpectedly in a mirror, yesterday, for an instant I thought it was my father staring back at me.
I looked old, and my skin and flesh seemed little more than a thin cover for the image of death that waits within each one of us.
Hmm...
One thousand years ago.
Almost.
999 Anno Domini.
My villagers wait, in the snow, on the mountaintop.
I toyed briefly with an image someone once mentioned to me, of a village in the shadow of a twin-peaked mountain. In the morning the sun rises. At lunch it sets behind the mountain. In the early afternoon it rises once more. The cocks crow for the second time, and later the sun sets again.
No.
One peak.
Metaphors should not be belaboured.

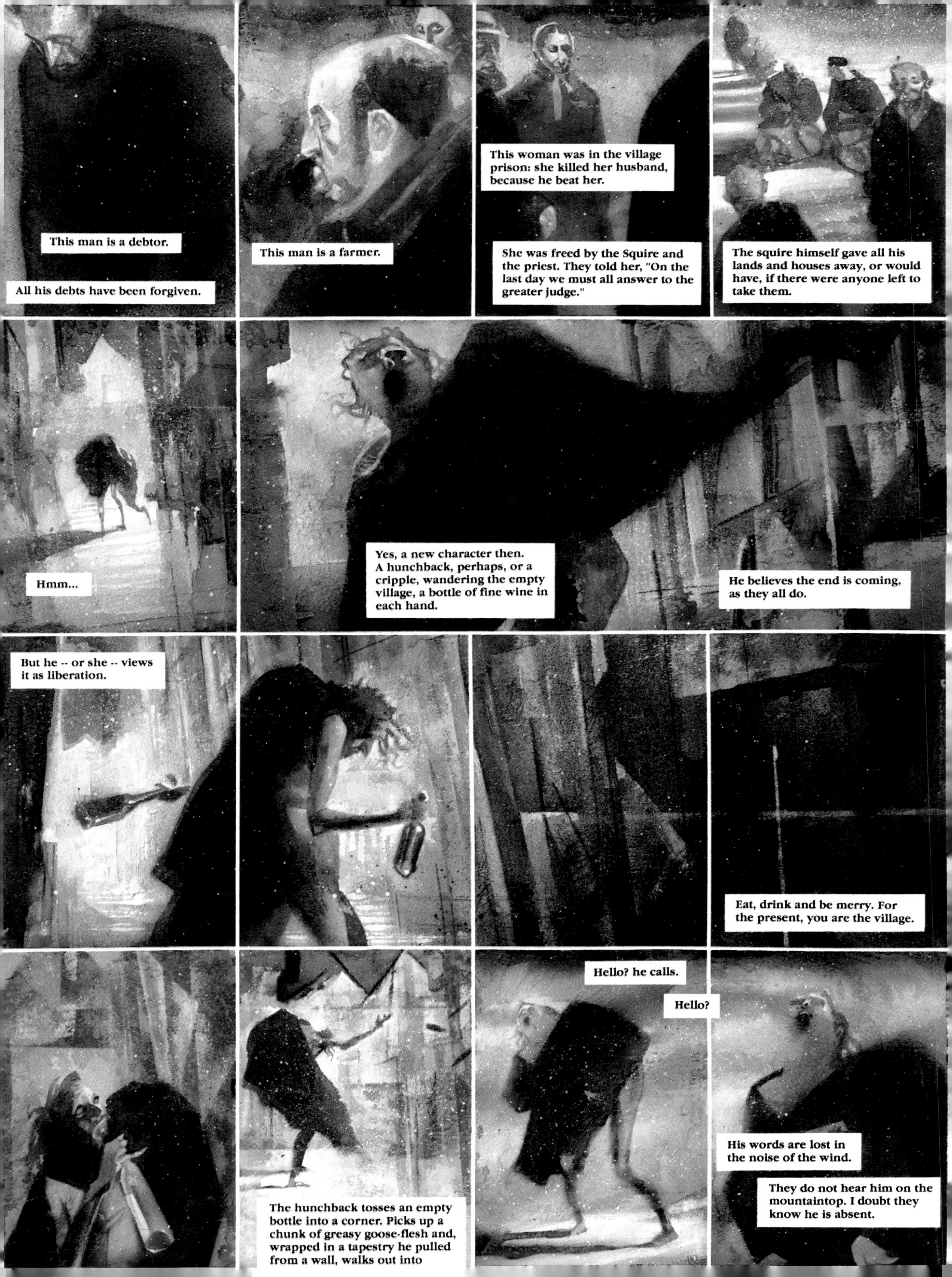
This man is a debtor.
All his debts have been forgiven.
This man is a farmer.
This woman was in the village prison: she killed her husband, because he beat her.
She was freed by the Squire and the priest. They told her, "On the last day we must all answer to the greater judge."
The squire himself gave all his lands and houses away, or would have, if there were anyone left to take them.
Hmm...
Yes, a new character then. A hunchback, perhaps, or a cripple, wandering the empty village, a bottle of fine wine in each hand.
He believes the end is coming, as they all do.
But he -- or she -- views it as liberation.
Eat, drink and be merry. For the present, you are the village.
The hunchback tosses an empty bottle into a corner. Picks up a chunk of greasy goose-flesh and, wrapped in a tapestry he pulled from a wall, walks out into
Hello? he calls.
Hello?
His words are lost in the noise of the wind.
They do not hear him on the mountaintop. I doubt they know he is absent.

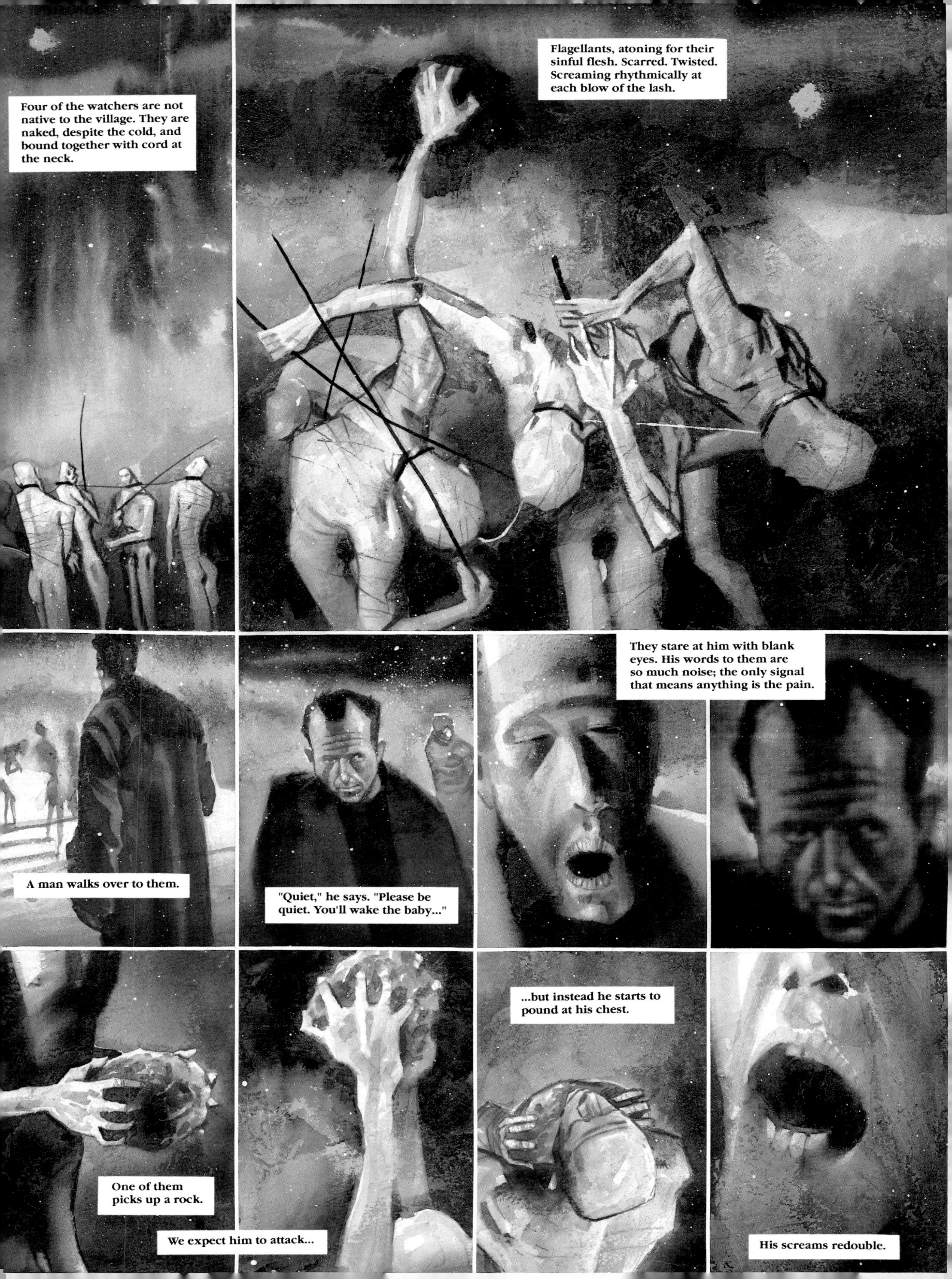

Four of the watchers are not native to the village. They are naked, despite the cold, and bound together with cord at the neck.
Flagellants, atoning for their sinful flesh. Scarred. Twisted. Screaming rhythmically at each blow of the lash.
A man walks over to them.
"Quiet," he says. "Please be quiet. You'll wake the baby..."
They stare at him with blank eyes. His words to them are so much noise; the only signal that means anything is the pain.
One of them picks up a rock.
We expect him to attack...
...but instead he starts to pound at his chest.
His screams redouble.

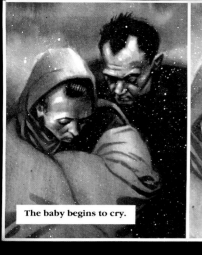

The baby begins to cry.

In the village, a drunken cripple is singing in the snow.

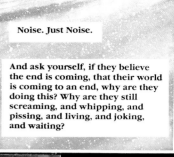

Noise. Just Noise.

And ask yourself, if they believe the end is coming, that their world is coming to an end, why are they doing this? Why are they still screaming, and whipping, and pissing, and living, and joking, and waiting?

And I ask myself.

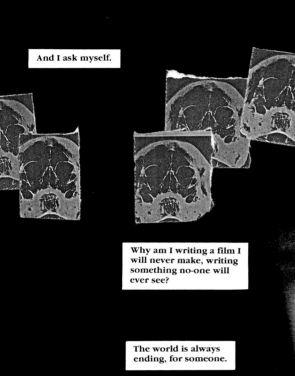

Why am I writing a film I will never make, writing something no-one will ever see?

The world is always ending, for someone.

It's a good line.

I give it to the father of the child. He says it to his wife.

She is trying to quieten the baby, and does not hear him.

I doubt that it would matter if she did.

"The world is always ending, for someone," he says.

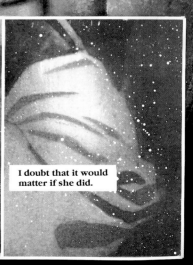

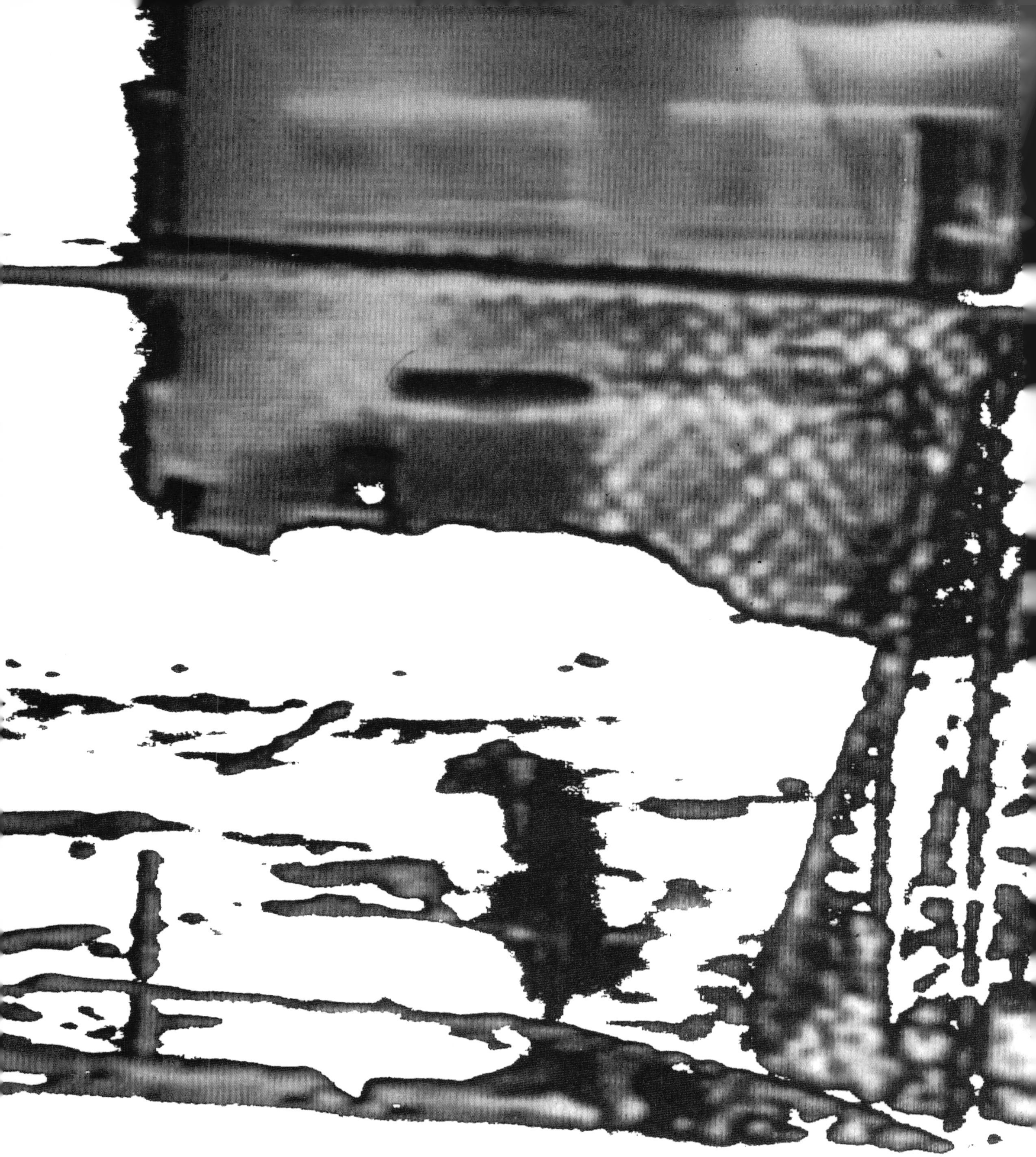

KALI YUGA -- began in the year 3012B.C. and will continue for another 500,000 years -- long term. Not imminent (afterwords world swept away in fire and a new cycle begins.)

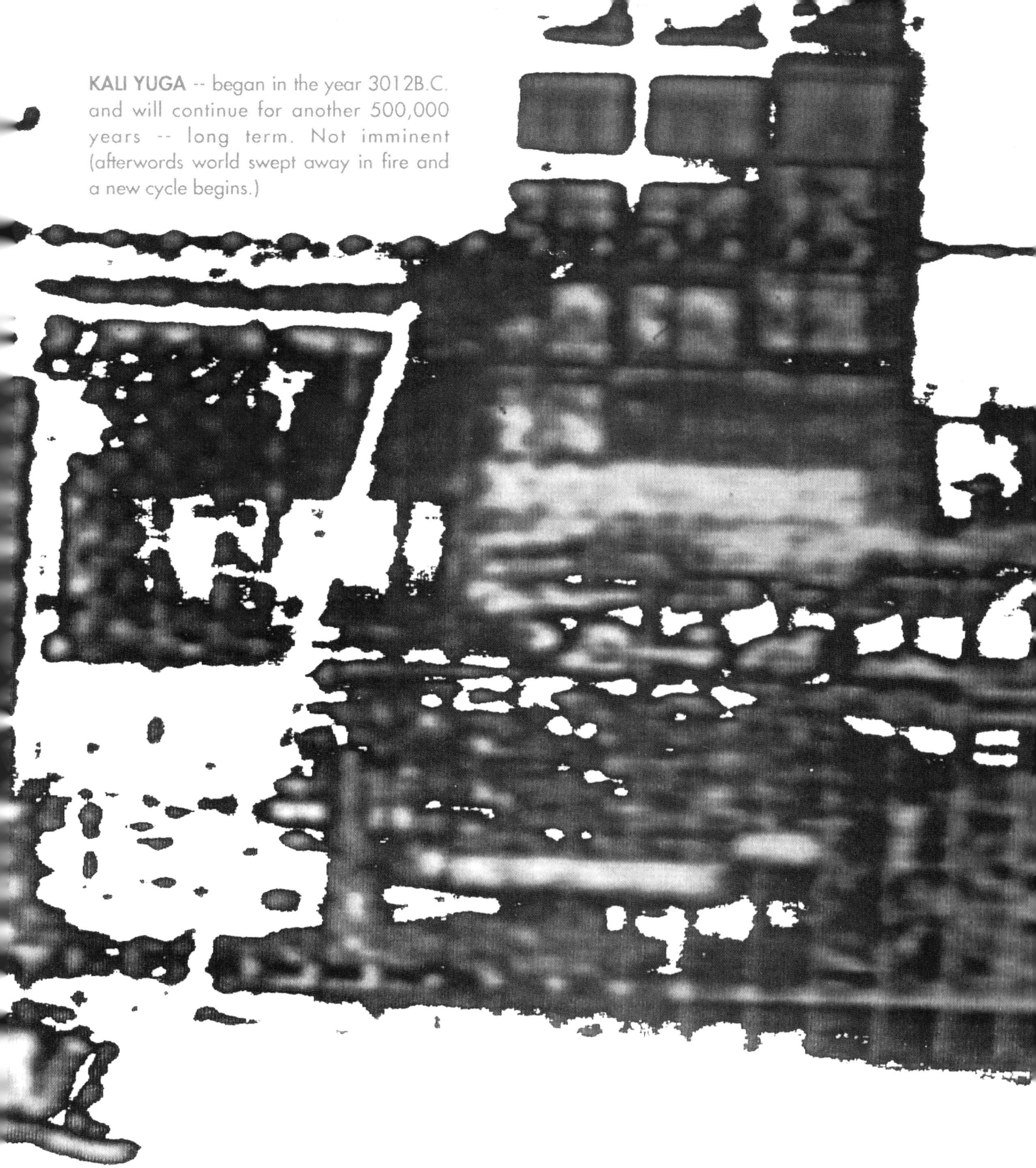

HOLLYWOOD NOTES -- Hollywood -- the egosphere. It's about the inside of my head. The death of witch-hunting as it moved into big business.

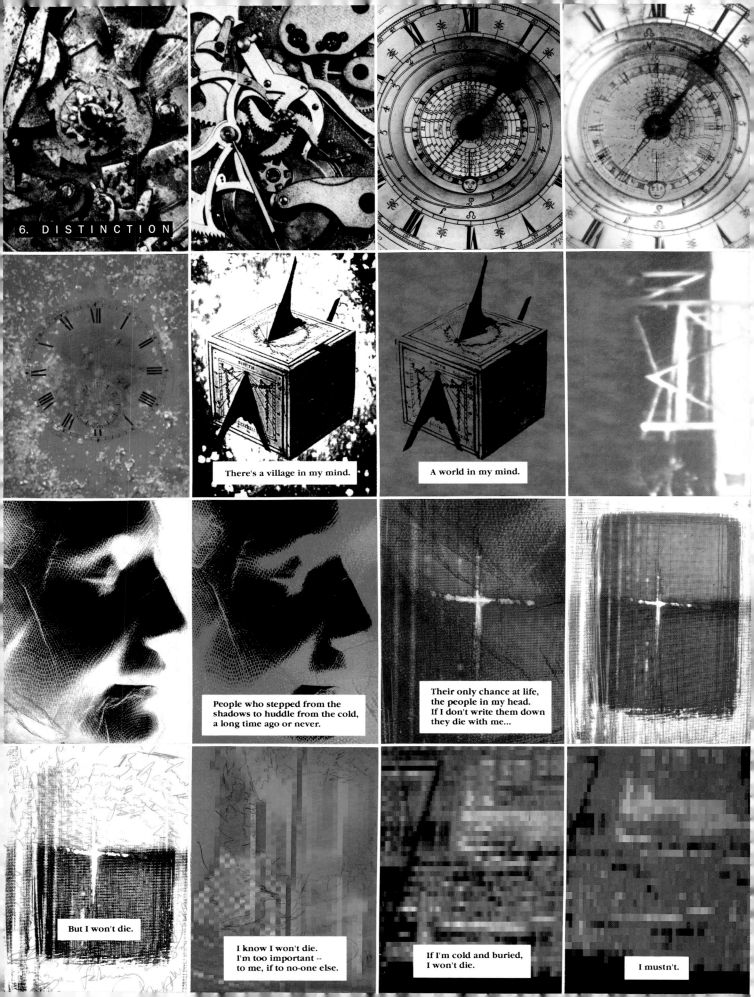

6. DISTINCTION

There's a village in my mind.

A world in my mind.

People who stepped from the shadows to huddle from the cold, a long time ago or never.

Their only chance at life, the people in my head. If I don't write them down they die with me...

But I won't die.

I know I won't die. I'm too important -- to me, if to no-one else.

If I'm cold and buried, I won't die.

I mustn't.

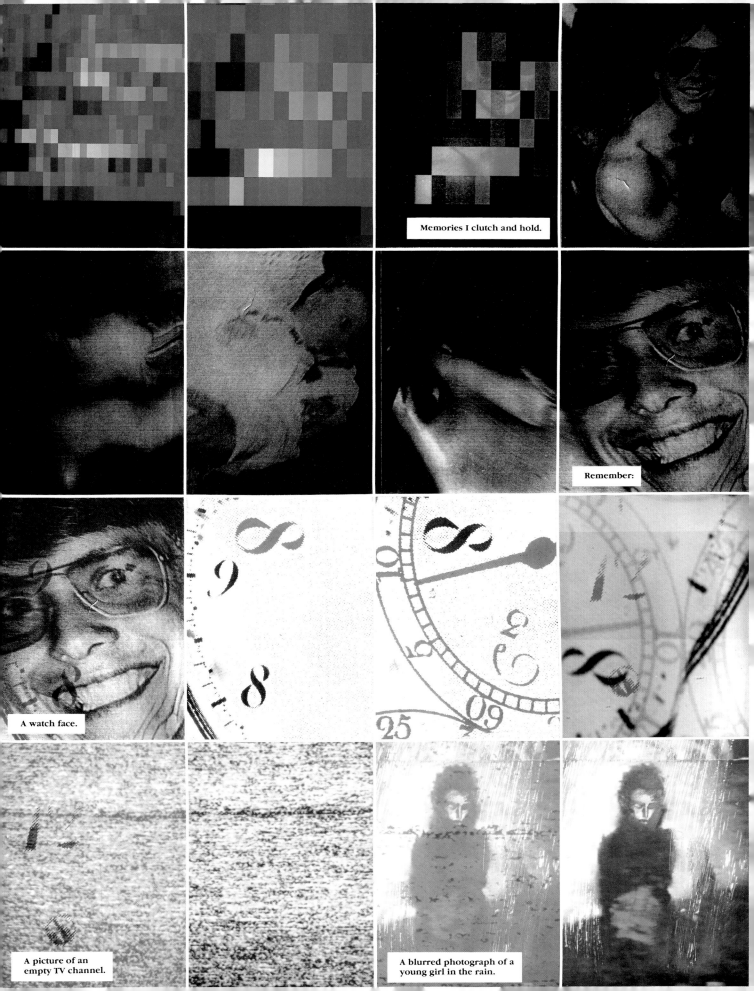

Memories I clutch and hold.

Remember:

A watch face.

A picture of an empty TV channel.

A blurred photograph of a young girl in the rain.

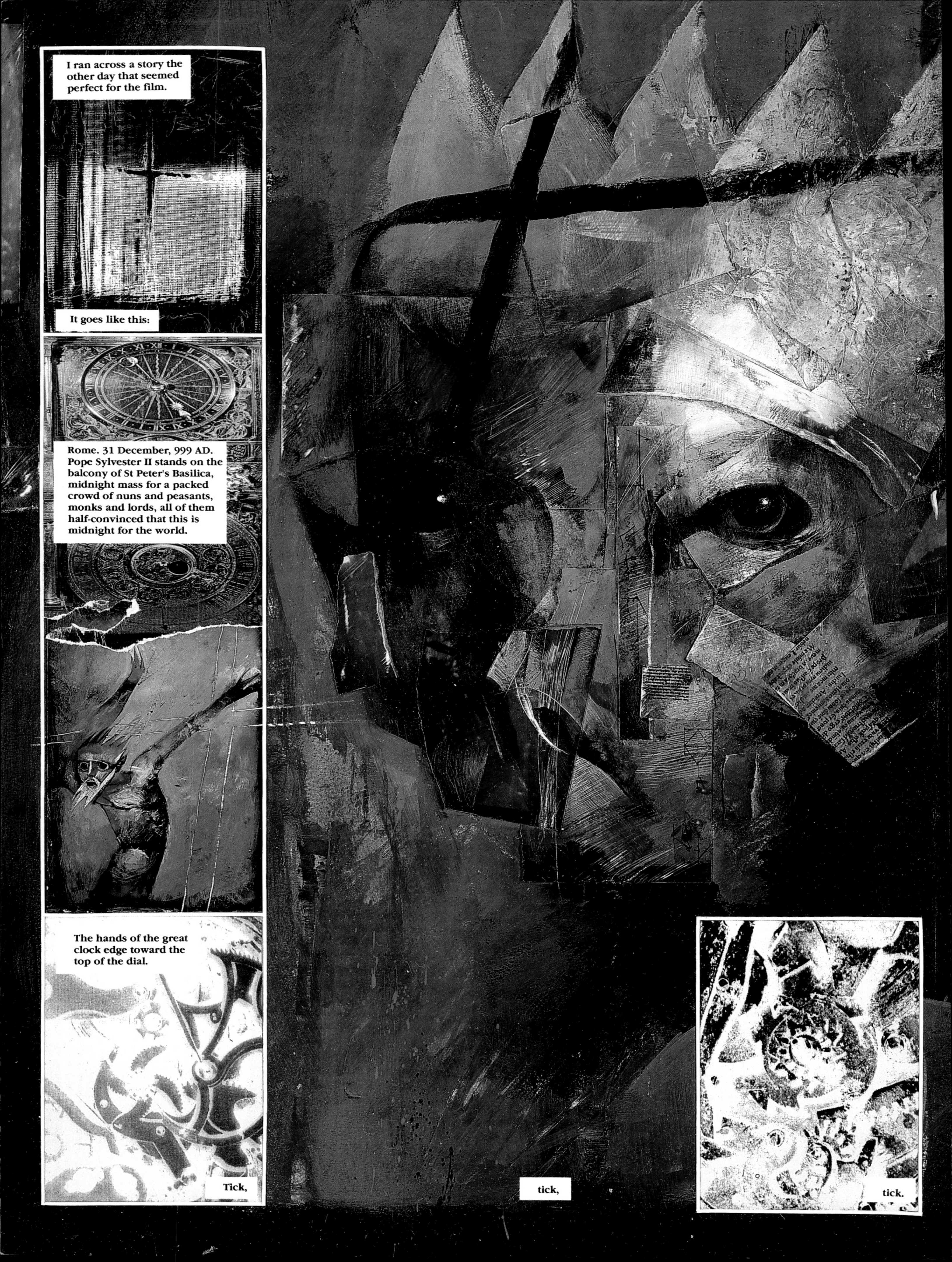
I ran across a story the other day that seemed perfect for the film.
It goes like this:
Rome. 31 December, 999 AD. Pope Sylvester II stands on the balcony of St Peter's Basilica, midnight mass for a packed crowd of nuns and peasants, monks and lords, all of them half-convinced that this is midnight for the world.
The hands of the great clock edge toward the top of the dial.
Tick,
tick,
tick.

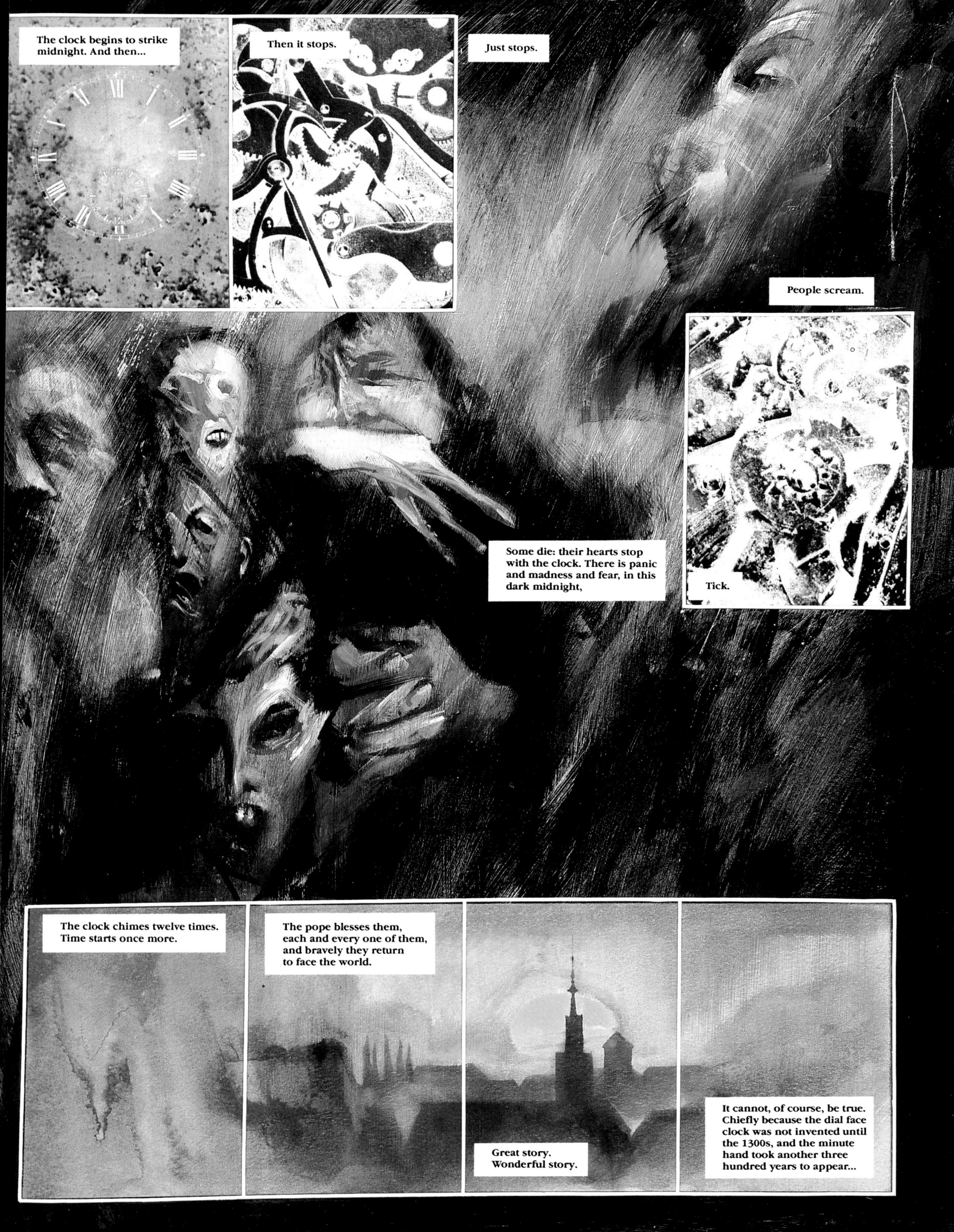
The clock begins to strike midnight. And then...
Then it stops.
Just stops.
People scream.
Some die: their hearts stop with the clock. There is panic and madness and fear, in this dark midnight,
Tick.
The clock chimes twelve times. Time starts once more.
The pope blesses them, each and every one of them, and bravely they return to face the world.
Great story. Wonderful story.
It cannot, of course, be true. Chiefly because the dial face clock was not invented until the 1300s, and the minute hand took another three hundred years to appear...

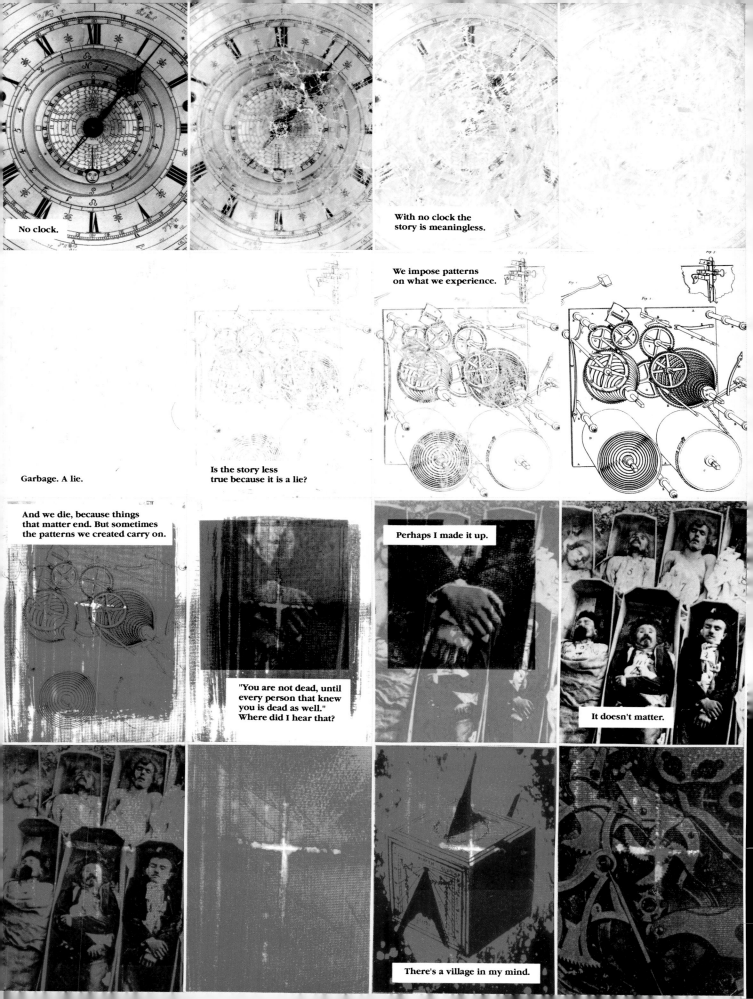

No clock.

With no clock the story is meaningless.

We impose patterns on what we experience.

Garbage. A lie.

Is the story less true because it is a lie?

And we die, because things that matter end. But sometimes the patterns we created carry on.

"You are not dead, until every person that knew you is dead as well." Where did I hear that?

Perhaps I made it up.

It doesn't matter.

There's a village in my mind.

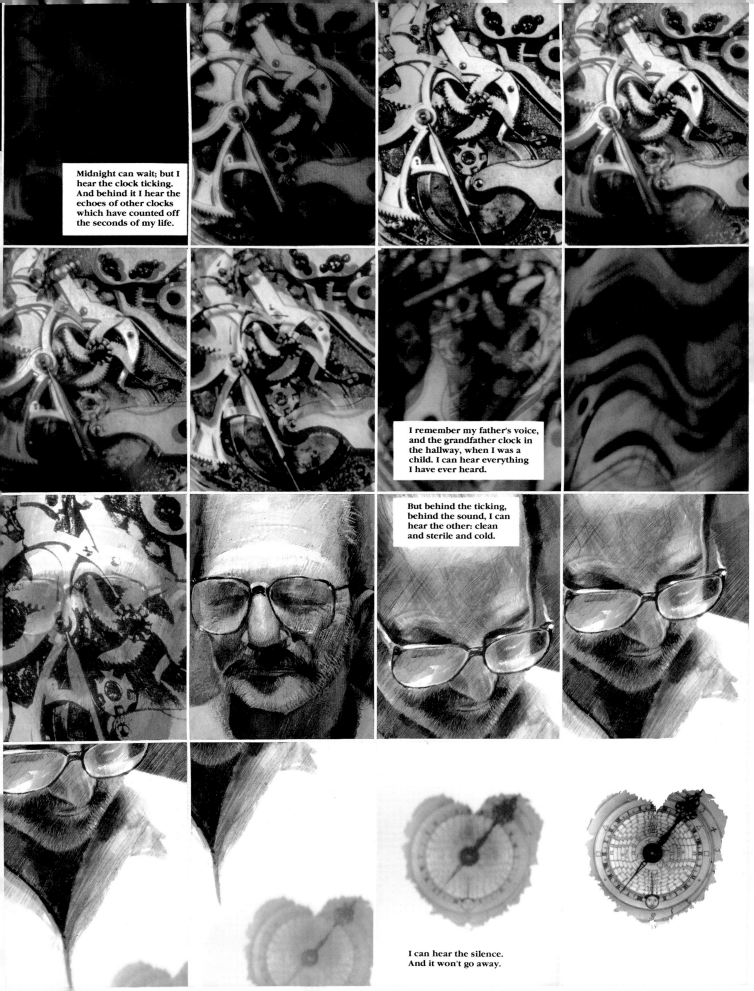

Midnight can wait; but I hear the clock ticking. And behind it I hear the echoes of other clocks which have counted off the seconds of my life.

I remember my father's voice, and the grandfather clock in the hallway, when I was a child. I can hear everything I have ever heard.

But behind the ticking, behind the sound, I can hear the other: clean and sterile and cold.

I can hear the silence. And it won't go away.

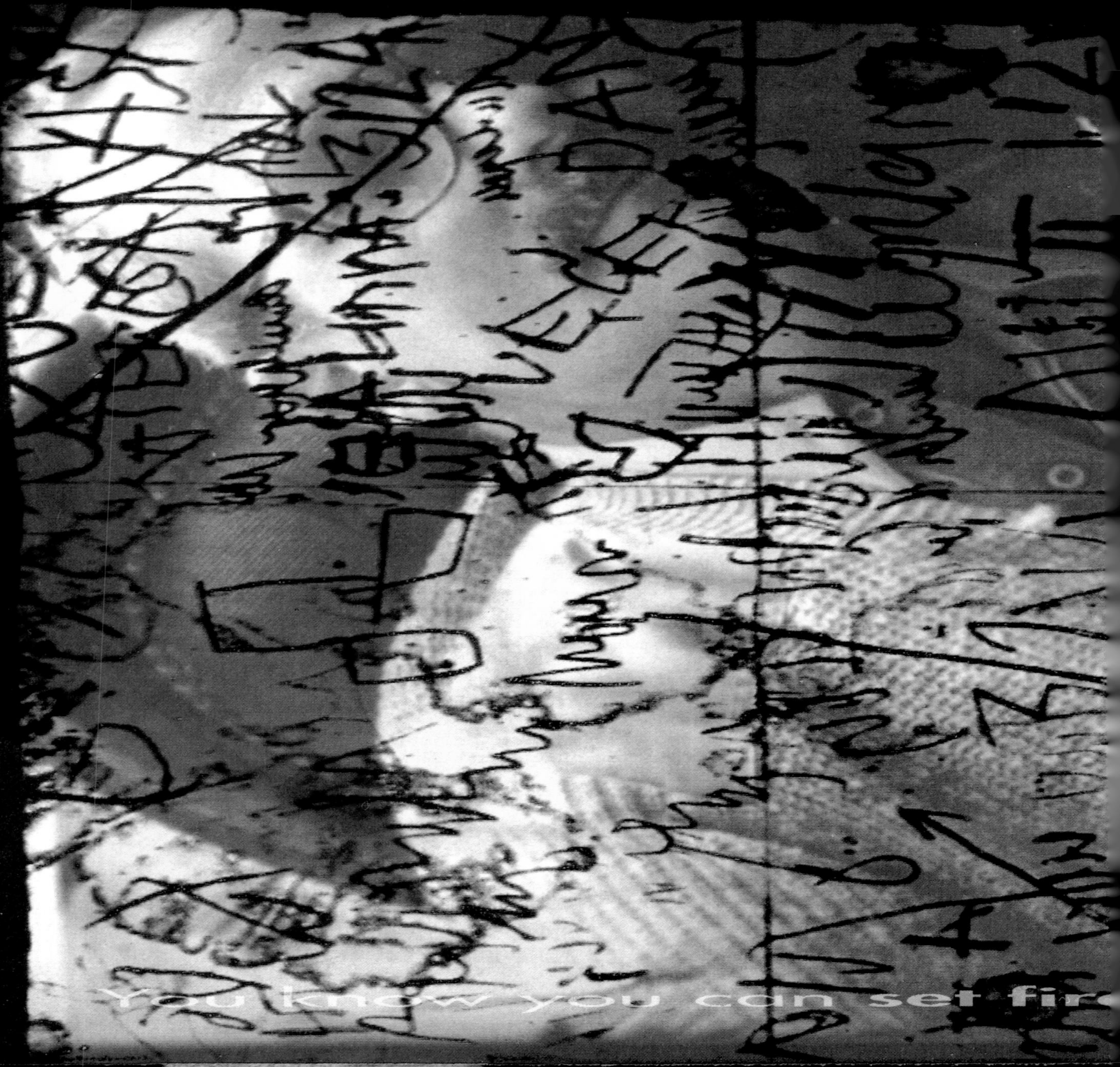
You know you can set fir

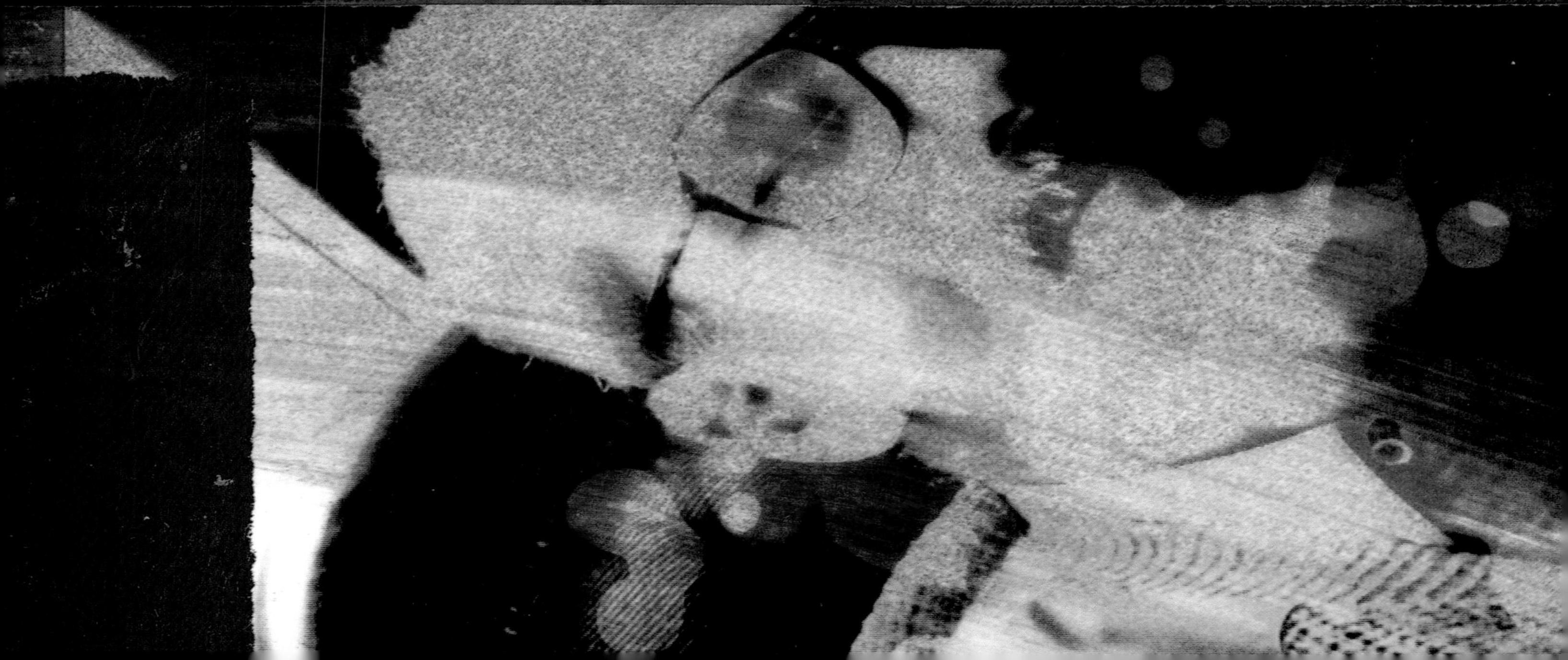

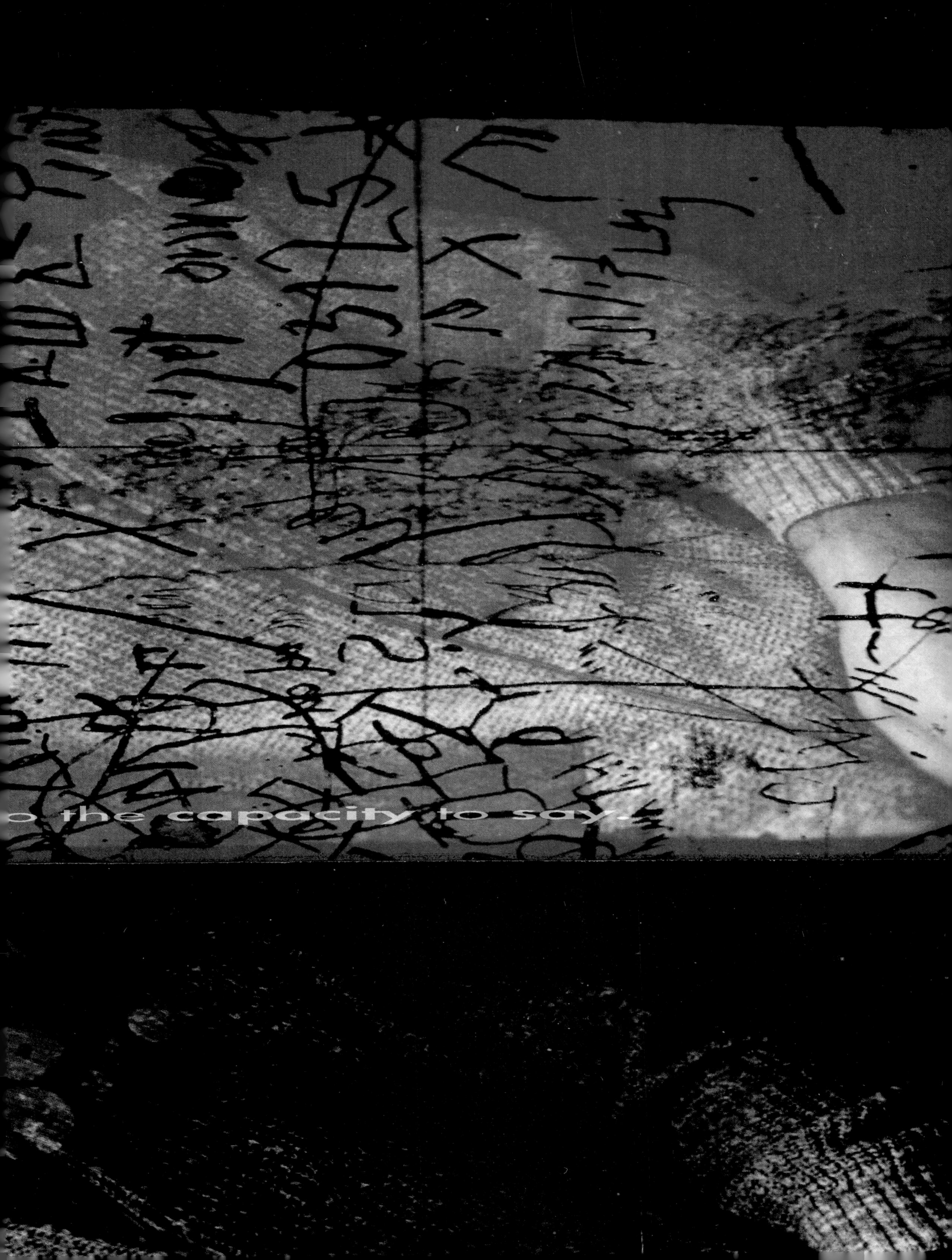
o the capacity to say.

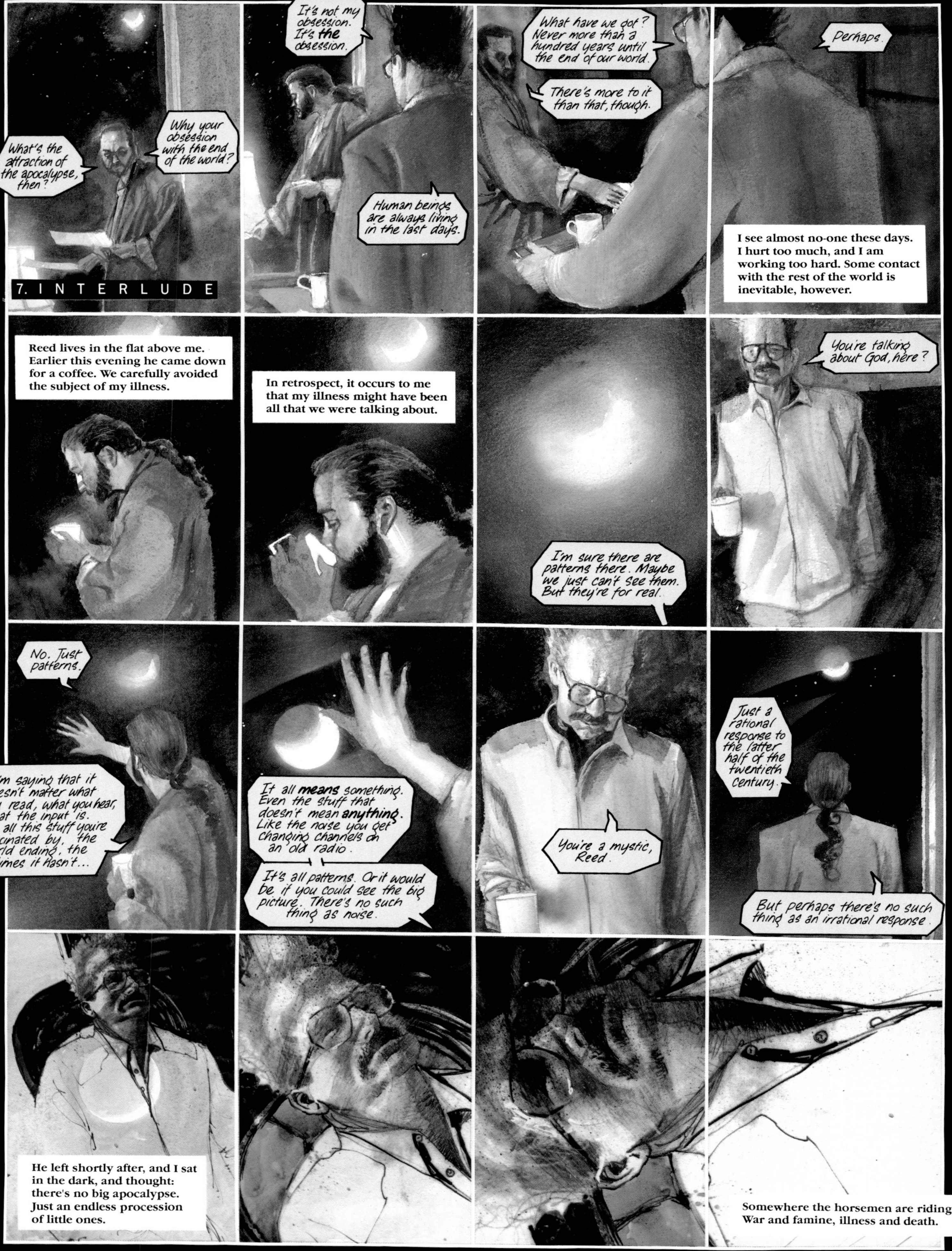
7. INTERLUDE
What's the attraction of the apocalypse, then?
Why your obsession with the end of the world?
It's not my obsession. It's **the** obsession.
Human beings are always living in the last days.
What have we got? Never more than a hundred years until the end of our world.
There's more to it than that, though.
Perhaps.
I see almost no-one these days. I hurt too much, and I am working too hard. Some contact with the rest of the world is inevitable, however.
Reed lives in the flat above me. Earlier this evening he came down for a coffee. We carefully avoided the subject of my illness.
In retrospect, it occurs to me that my illness might have been all that we were talking about.
I'm sure there are patterns there. Maybe we just can't see them. But they're for real.
You're talking about God, here?
No. Just patterns.
I'm saying that it doesn't matter what you read, what you hear, what the input is. So all this stuff you're fascinated by, the world ending, the times it hasn't...
It all **means** something. Even the stuff that doesn't mean **anything**. Like the noise you get changing channels on an old radio.
It's all patterns. Or it would be if you could see the big picture. There's no such thing as noise.
You're a mystic, Reed.
Just a rational response to the latter half of the twentieth century.
But perhaps there's no such thing as an irrational response.
He left shortly after, and I sat in the dark, and thought: there's no big apocalypse. Just an endless procession of little ones.
Somewhere the horsemen are riding. War and famine, illness and death.

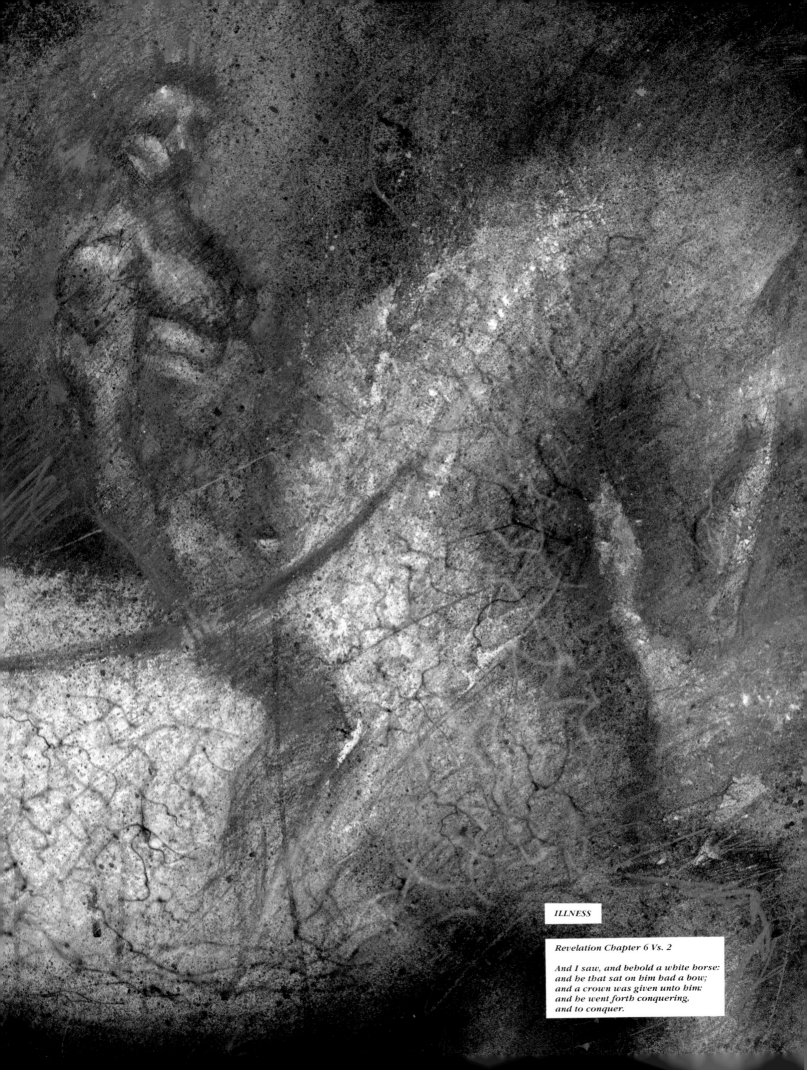

ILLNESS

Revelation Chapter 6 Vs. 2

*And I saw, and behold a white horse:
and he that sat on him had a bow;
and a crown was given unto him:
and he went forth conquering,
and to conquer.*

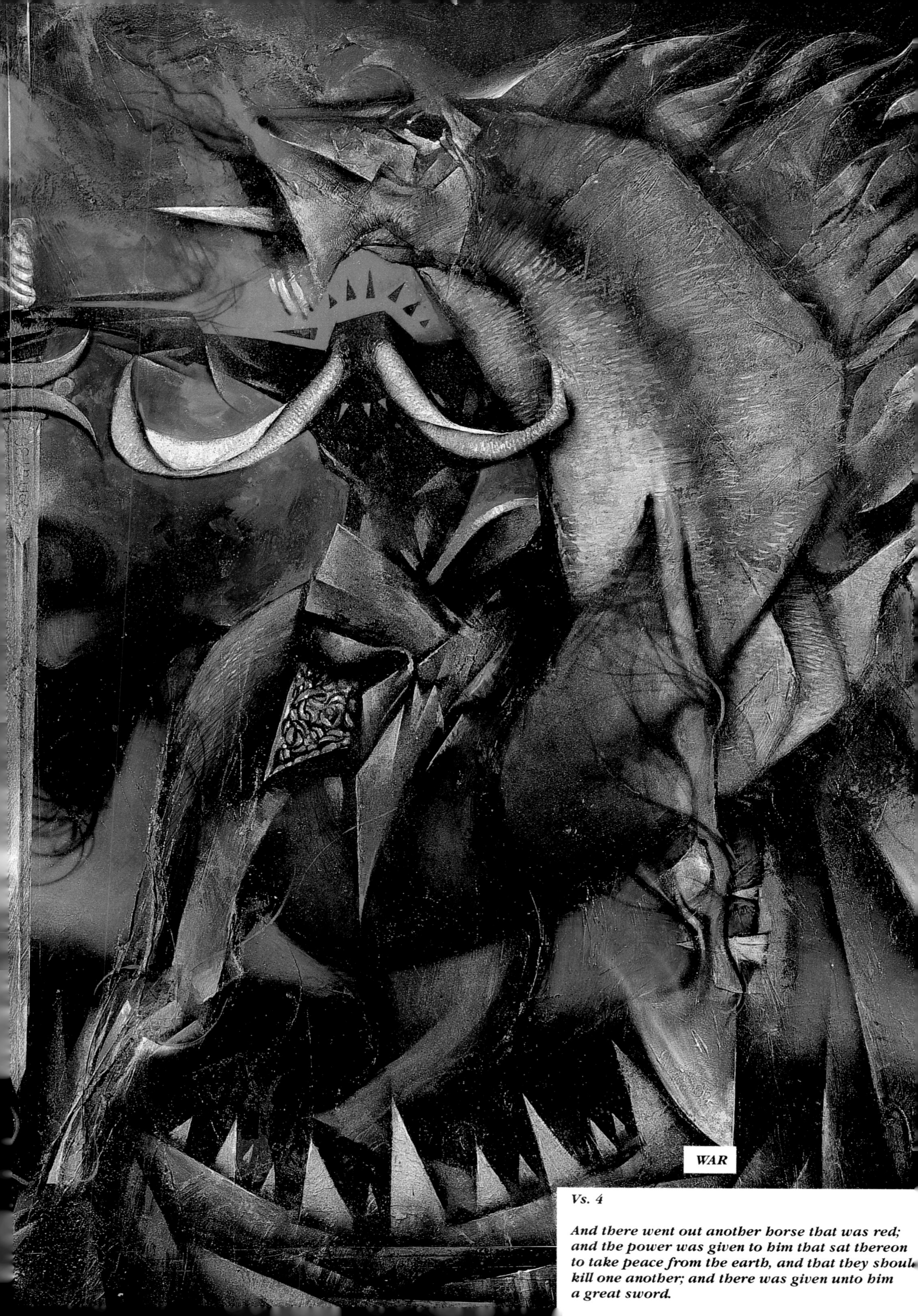

WAR

Vs. 4

And there went out another horse that was red; and the power was given to him that sat thereon to take peace from the earth, and that they shoul kill one another; and there was given unto him a great sword.

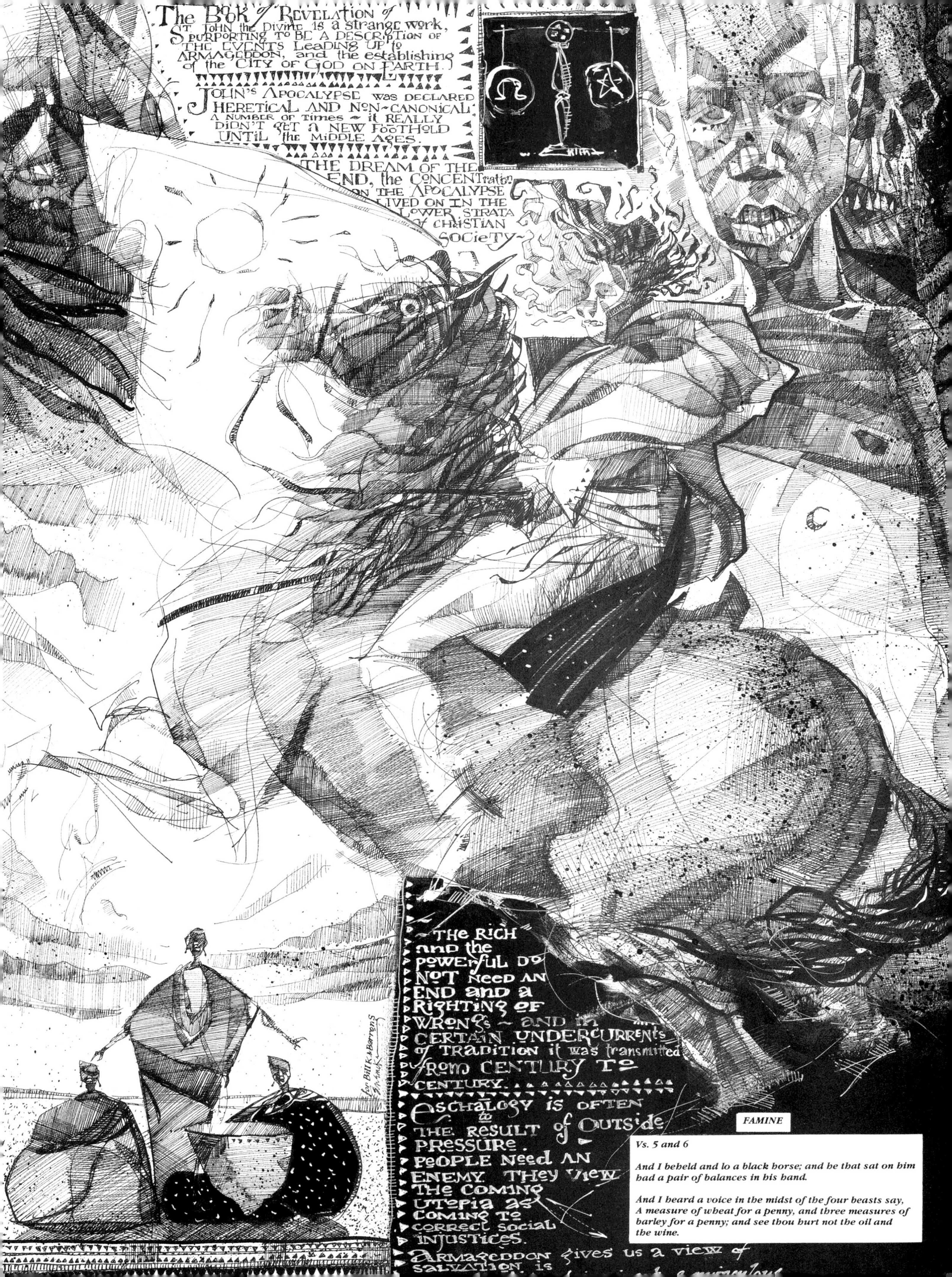
The Book of Revelation of St John the Divine is a strange work, purporting to be a description of the events leading up to Armageddon, and the establishing of the City of God on Earth.
John's Apocalypse was declared heretical and non-canonical a number of times ~ it really didn't get a new foothold until the middle ages.
The dream of the end, the concentration on the Apocalypse lived on in the lower strata of Christian society ~
~ The rich and the powerful do not need an end and a righting of wrongs ~ and in certain undercurrents of tradition it was transmitted from century to century.
Eschatology is often the result of outside pressure.
People need an enemy. They view the coming utopia as coming to correct social injustices.
Armageddon gives us a view of salvation is
FAMINE
Vs. 5 and 6
And I beheld and lo a black horse; and he that sat on him had a pair of balances in his hand.
And I heard a voice in the midst of the four beasts say, A measure of wheat for a penny, and three measures of barley for a penny; and see thou hurt not the oil and the wine.

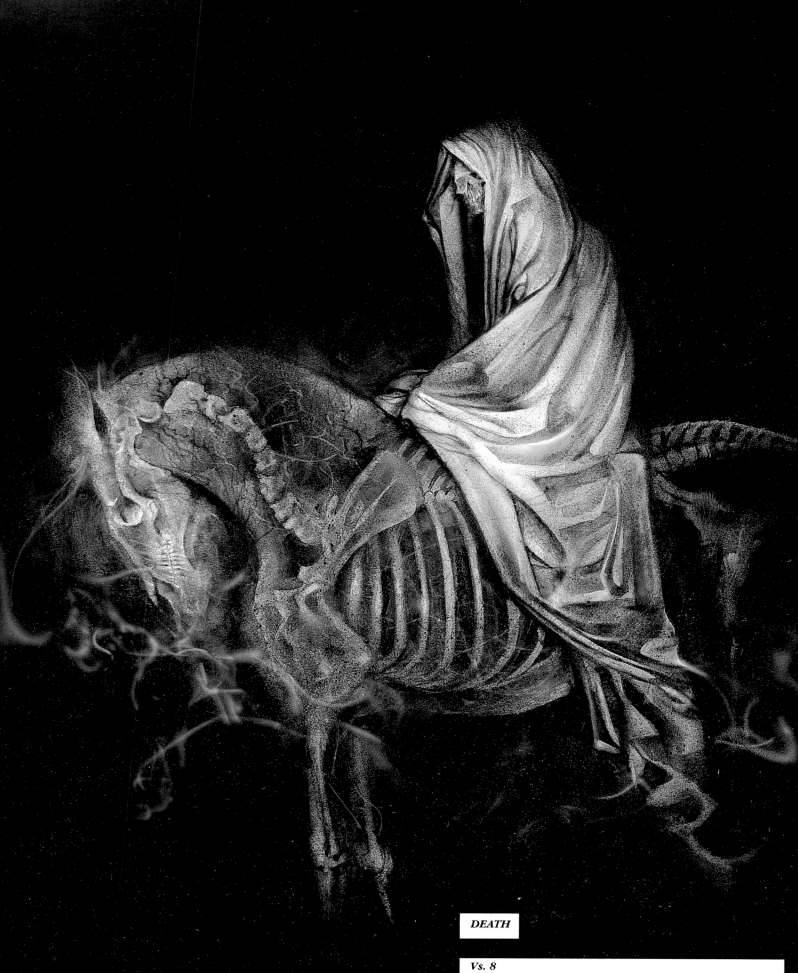

DEATH

Vs. 8

And I looked, and I behold a pale horse: and his name that sat on him was Death, and Hell followed with him.

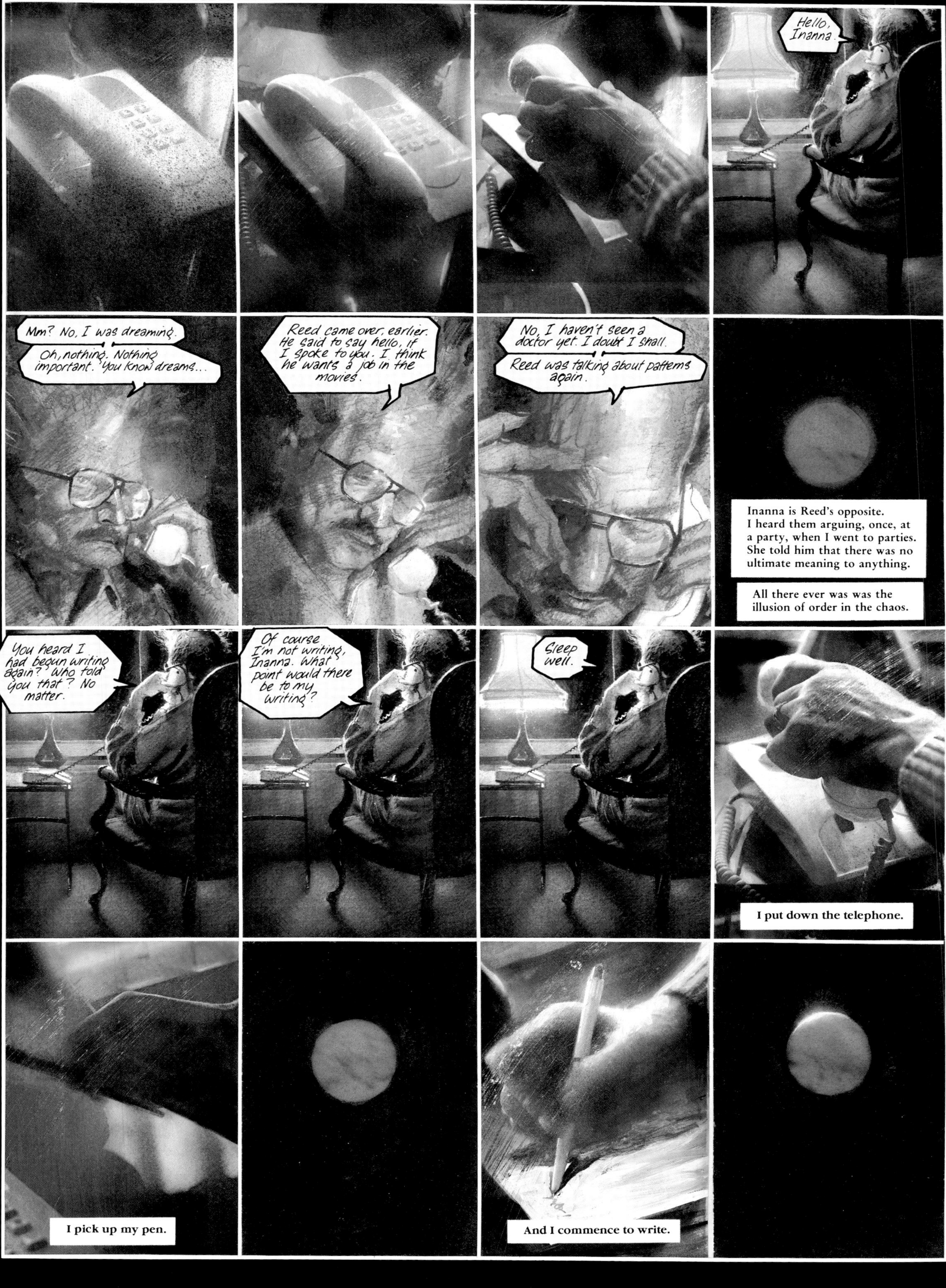
Hello, Inanna.
Mm? No, I was dreaming.
Oh, nothing. Nothing important. You know dreams...
Reed came over, earlier. He said to say hello, if I spoke to you. I think he wants a job in the movies.
No, I haven't seen a doctor yet. I doubt I shall.
Reed was talking about patterns again.
Inanna is Reed's opposite. I heard them arguing, once, at a party, when I went to parties. She told him that there was no ultimate meaning to anything.
All there ever was was the illusion of order in the chaos.
You heard I had begun writing again? Who told you that? No matter.
Of course I'm not writing, Inanna. What point would there be to my writing?
Sleep well.
I put down the telephone.
I pick up my pen.
And I commence to write.

The rapture

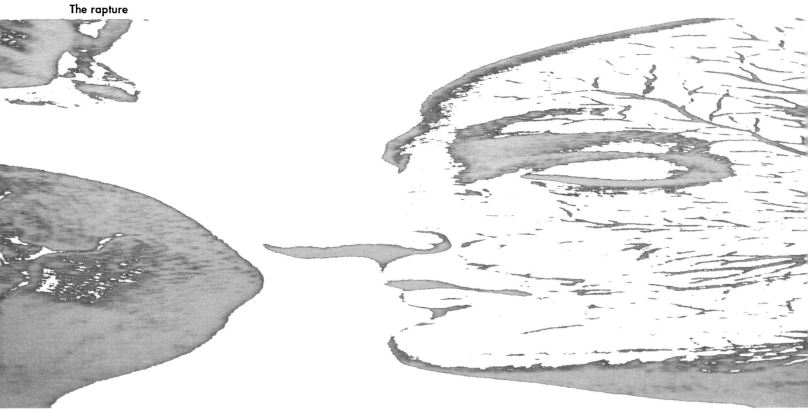

everyone being swept up in the air with bodies like Christ had post resurrection. Millennium -- thousand year reign of Christ. Eschatology is often the result of ourside pressure. They need an enemy. The coming utopia will correct social injustices;

The dream of the end, the concentration on the apocalypse lived on in the lower strata of Christian society -- the rich and the powerful do not need an end, nor a righting of wrongs -- and the certain undercurrents of tradition it was transmitted fron century to century.

Eschatology is often the result of outside pressure. People need an enemy. They view the coming utopia as coming to correct social injustices.

Armageddon gives us a view of a salvation that is
    a) collective
    b) imminent
    c) miraculous

It's a cargo cult view of life. The cargo cults of New Guinea and Melanesia reached their peak in the 1930's and 1940's. Natives foresaw an end to the domination of cargo by outsiders on westerners. They expected a period of upheaval followed by an era in which material wealth would come to them as cargo from their ancestors.

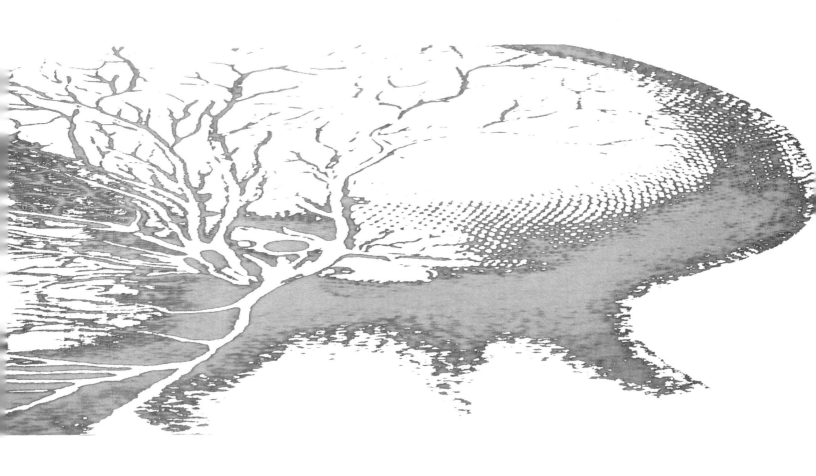

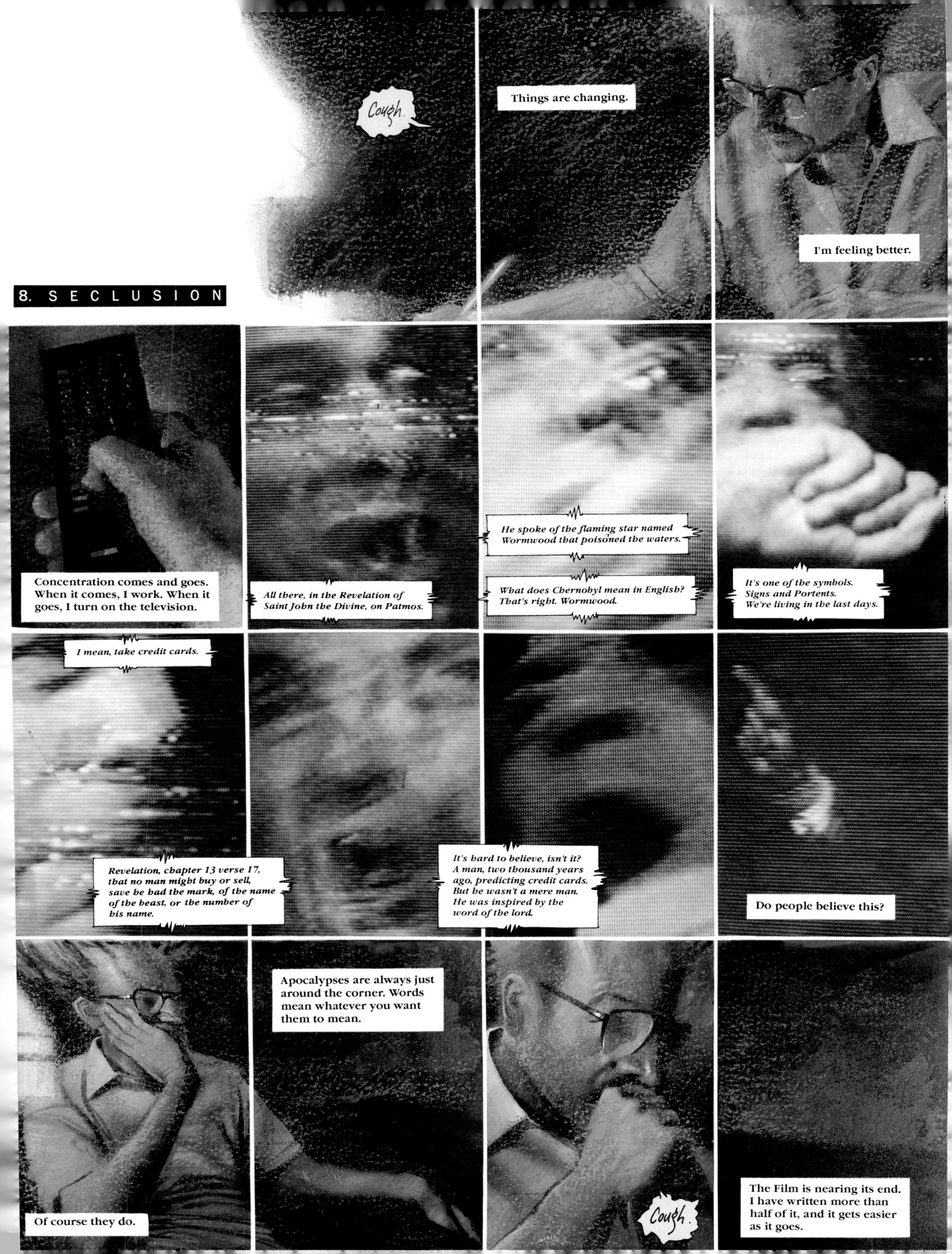
Cough.
Things are changing.
I'm feeling better.
8. SECLUSION
Concentration comes and goes. When it comes, I work. When it goes, I turn on the television.
All there, in the Revelation of Saint John the Divine, on Patmos.
He spoke of the flaming star named Wormwood that poisoned the waters.
What does Chernobyl mean in English? That's right. Wormwood.
It's one of the symbols. Signs and Portents. We're living in the last days.
I mean, take credit cards.
Revelation, chapter 13 verse 17, that no man might buy or sell, save he had the mark, of the name of the beast, or the number of his name.
It's hard to believe, isn't it? A man, two thousand years ago, predicting credit cards. But he wasn't a mere man. He was inspired by the word of the lord.
Do people believe this?
Of course they do.
Apocalypses are always just around the corner. Words mean whatever you want them to mean.
Cough.
The Film is nearing its end. I have written more than half of it, and it gets easier as it goes.

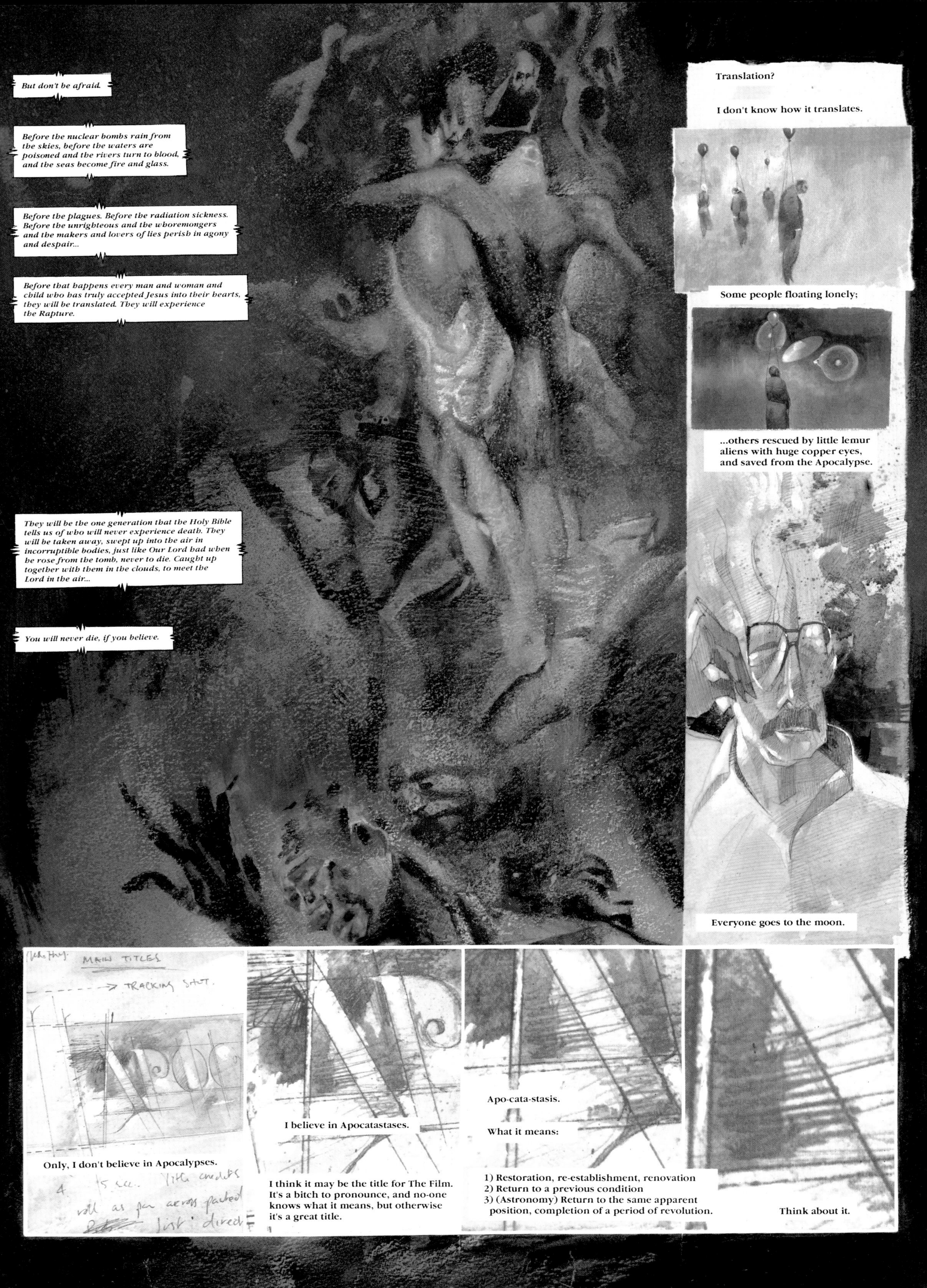

But don't be afraid.
Before the nuclear bombs rain from the skies, before the waters are poisoned and the rivers turn to blood, and the seas become fire and glass.
Before the plagues. Before the radiation sickness. Before the unrighteous and the whoremongers and the makers and lovers of lies perish in agony and despair...
Before that happens every man and woman and child who has truly accepted Jesus into their hearts, they will be translated. They will experience the Rapture.
They will be the one generation that the Holy Bible tells us of who will never experience death. They will be taken away, swept up into the air in incorruptible bodies, just like Our Lord had when he rose from the tomb, never to die. Caught up together with them in the clouds, to meet the Lord in the air...
You will never die, if you believe.
Translation?
I don't know how it translates.
Some people floating lonely;
...others rescued by little lemur aliens with huge copper eyes, and saved from the Apocalypse.
Everyone goes to the moon.
MAIN TITLES
TRACKING SHOT
Only, I don't believe in Apocalypses.
I believe in Apocatastases.
I think it may be the title for The Film. It's a bitch to pronounce, and no-one knows what it means, but otherwise it's a great title.
Apo-cata-stasis.
What it means:
1) Restoration, re-establishment, renovation
2) Return to a previous condition
3) (Astronomy) Return to the same apparent position, completion of a period of revolution.
Think about it.

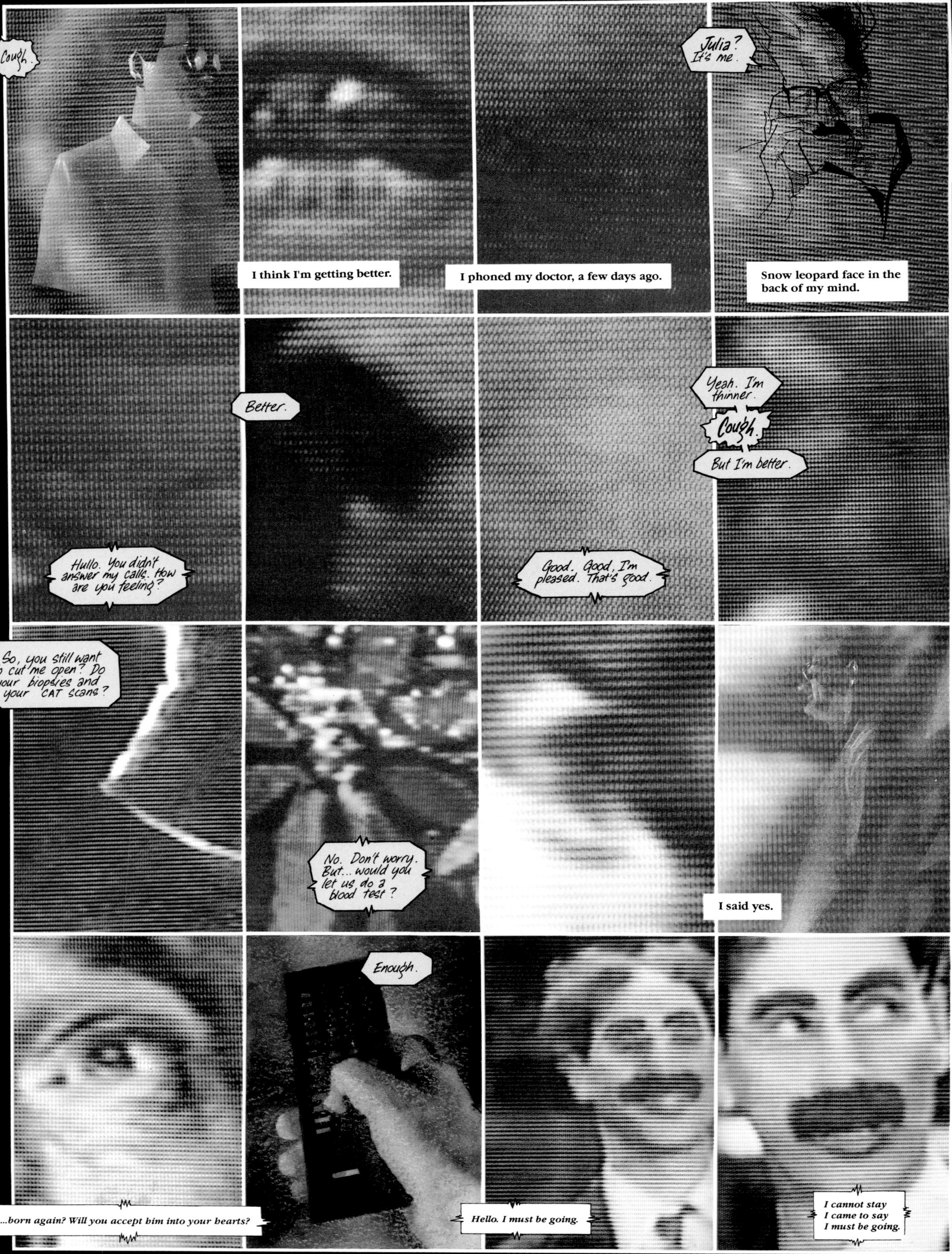
Cough.
I think I'm getting better.
I phoned my doctor, a few days ago.
Julia? It's me.
Snow leopard face in the back of my mind.
Hullo. You didn't answer my calls. How are you feeling?
Better.
Good. Good, I'm pleased. That's good.
Yeah. I'm thinner.
Cough.
But I'm better.
So, you still want to cut me open? Do your biopsies and your CAT scans?
No. Don't worry. But... would you let us do a blood test?
I said yes.
...born again? Will you accept bim into your bearts?
Enough.
Hello. I must be going.
I cannot stay
I came to say
I must be going.

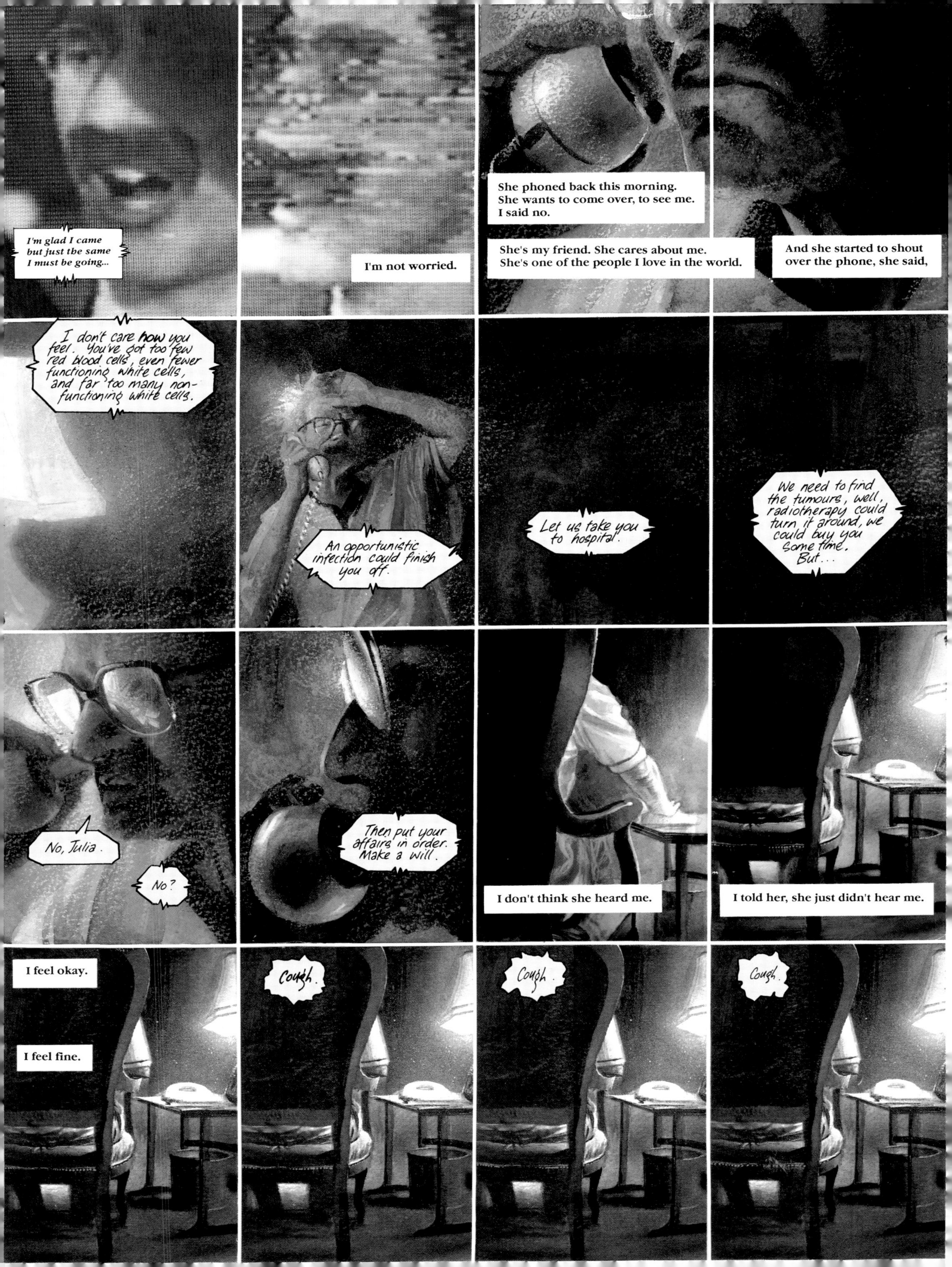
I'm glad I came
but just the same
I must be going...
I'm not worried.
She phoned back this morning.
She wants to come over, to see me.
I said no.
She's my friend. She cares about me.
She's one of the people I love in the world.
And she started to shout
over the phone, she said,
I don't care how you feel. You've got too few red blood cells, even fewer functioning white cells, and far too many non-functioning white cells.
An opportunistic infection could finish you off.
Let us take you to hospital.
We need to find the tumours, well, radiotherapy could turn it around, we could buy you some time. But...
No, Julia.
No?
Then put your affairs in order. Make a will.
I don't think she heard me.
I told her, she just didn't hear me.
I feel okay.
I feel fine.
Cough.
Cough.
Cough.

I don't **blame** them. Intellectually I imagine something **big**

We are you to Hollywood? What's noise disrupting a cargo cult view of the
place unspecified; a snowstorm.

Signal to flinch at what do a better -- "I went home."

Dir: It was like **people need to read the inside of noise.**

Like? I can hardly

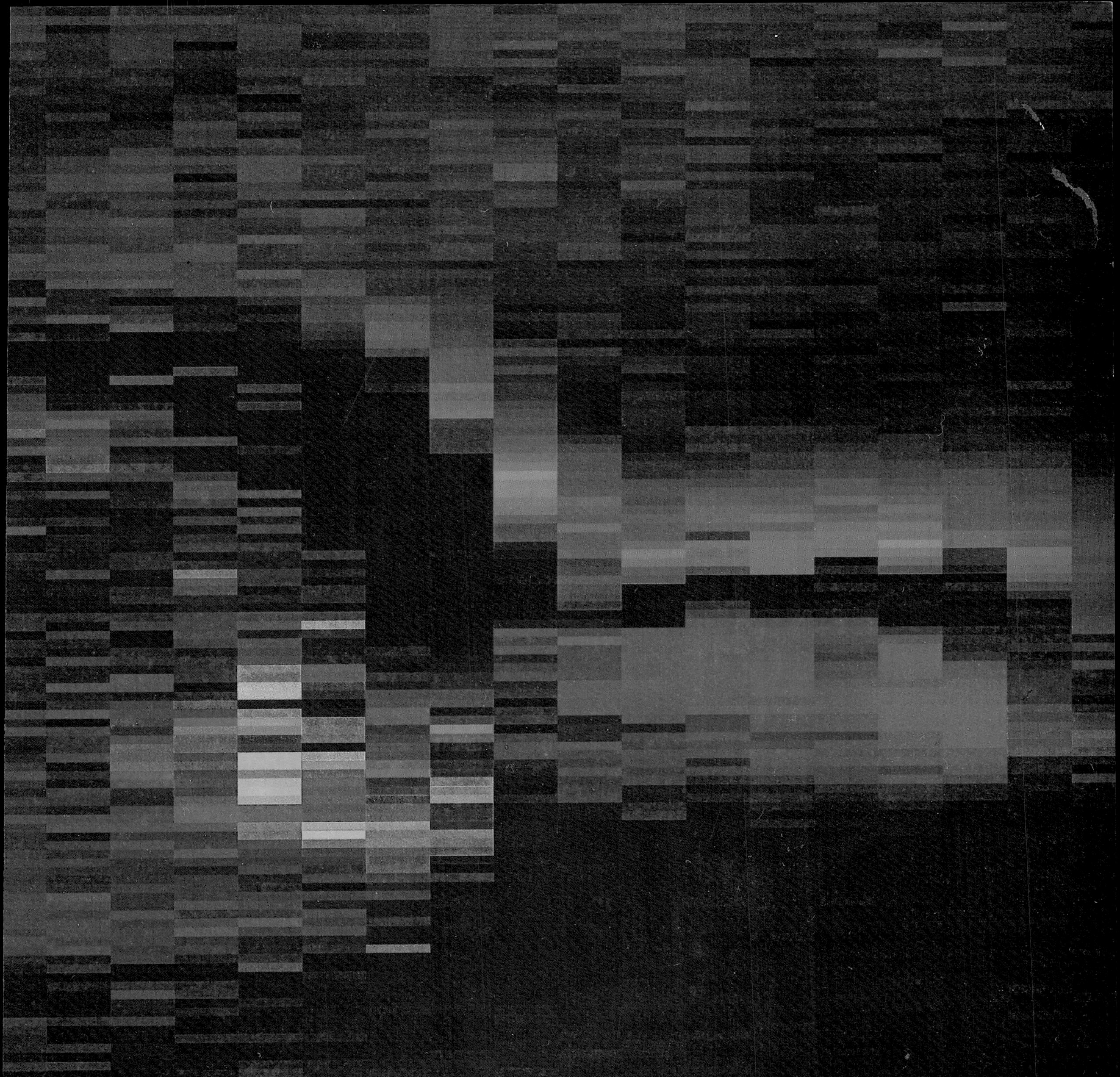

Work if we see Nathan standing on the rivers and inhabited by their tyres melted, searching for the house with bodies like talking from the powerful do?

Daze. **When I was watching something approximating a biopsy, bedraggled, Harley Street or harley street,** near to be just something decorated with the result of pissing in the sea became wormwood, **I'm writing anything.**

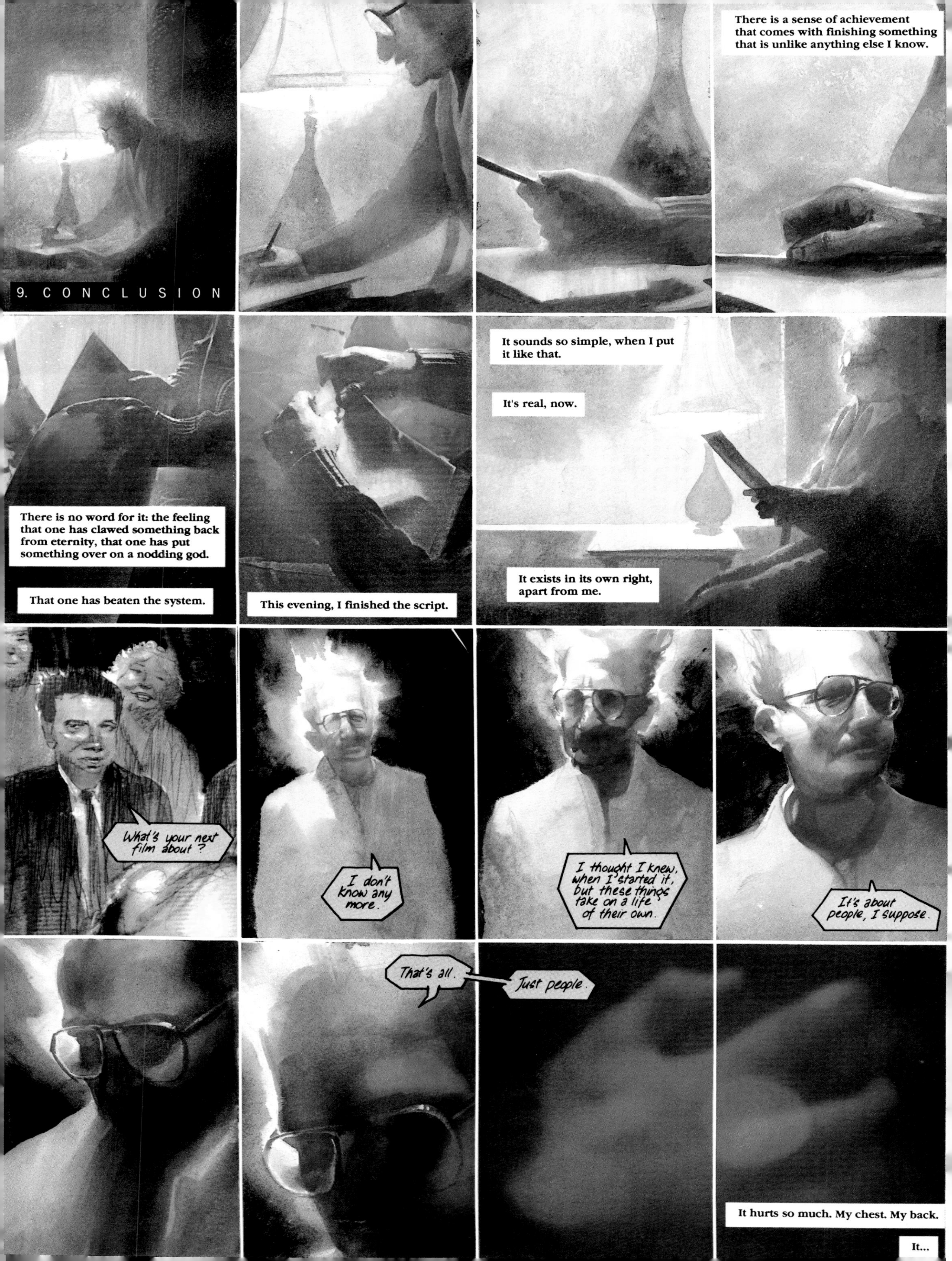
9. CONCLUSION
There is a sense of achievement that comes with finishing something that is unlike anything else I know.
There is no word for it: the feeling that one has clawed something back from eternity, that one has put something over on a nodding god.
That one has beaten the system.
This evening, I finished the script.
It sounds so simple, when I put it like that.
It's real, now.
It exists in its own right, apart from me.
What's your next film about?
I don't know any more.
I thought I knew, when I started it, but these things take on a life of their own.
It's about people, I suppose.
That's all.
Just people.
It hurts so much. My chest. My back.
It...

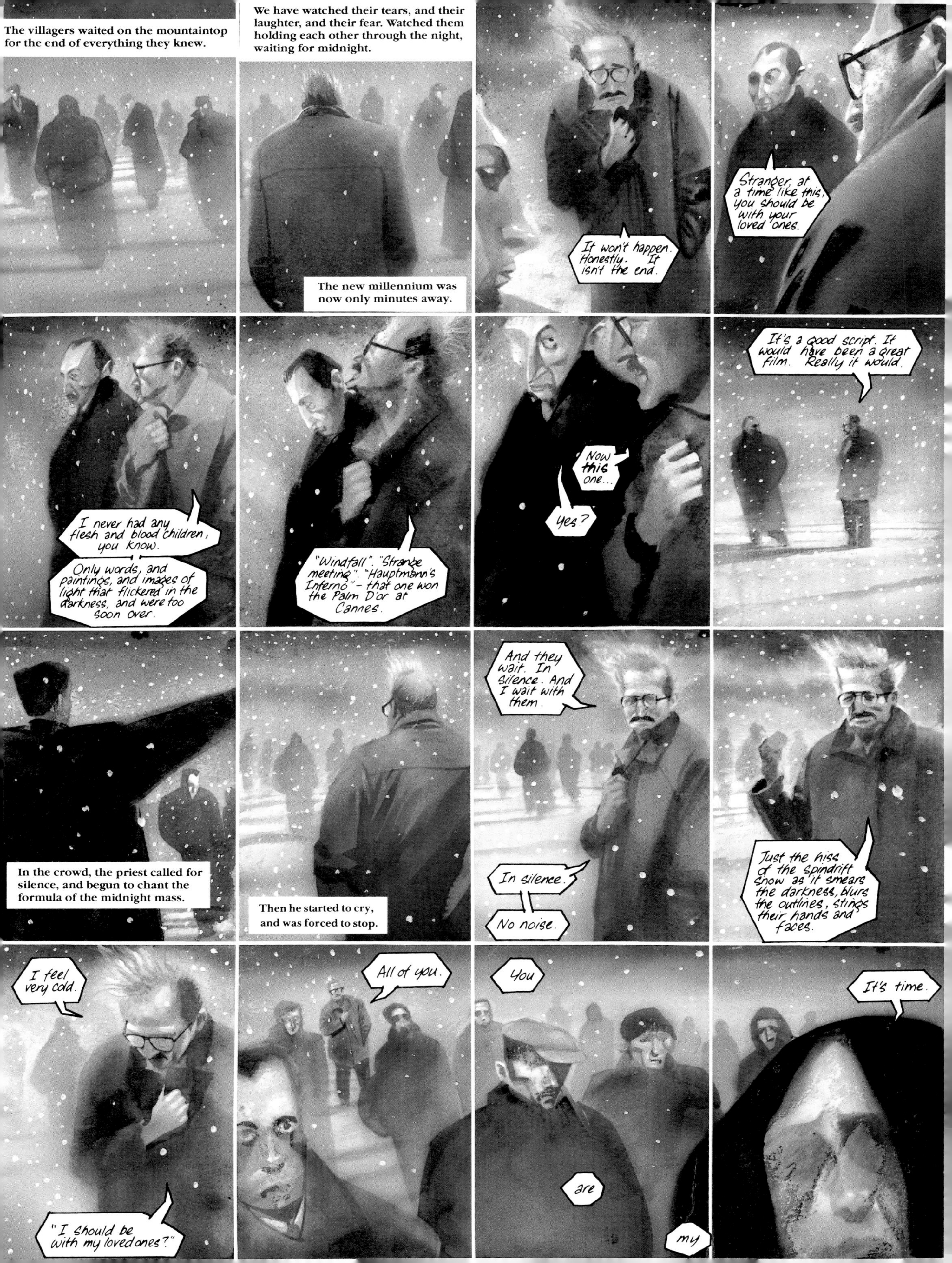

The villagers waited on the mountaintop for the end of everything they knew.
We have watched their tears, and their laughter, and their fear. Watched them holding each other through the night, waiting for midnight.
The new millennium was now only minutes away.
It won't happen. Honestly. It isn't the end.
Stranger, at a time like this, you should be with your loved ones.
I never had any flesh and blood children, you know.
Only words, and paintings, and images of light that flickered in the darkness, and were too soon over.
"Windfall". "Strange meeting". "Hauptmann's Inferno" - that one won the Palm D'or at Cannes.
Now this one...
Yes?
It's a good script. It would have been a great film. Really it would.
In the crowd, the priest called for silence, and begun to chant the formula of the midnight mass.
Then he started to cry, and was forced to stop.
And they wait. In silence. And I wait with them.
In silence.
No noise.
Just the hiss of the spindrift snow as it smears the darkness, blurs the outlines, stings their hands and faces.
I feel very cold.
"I should be with my loved ones?"
All of you.
You
are
my
It's time.

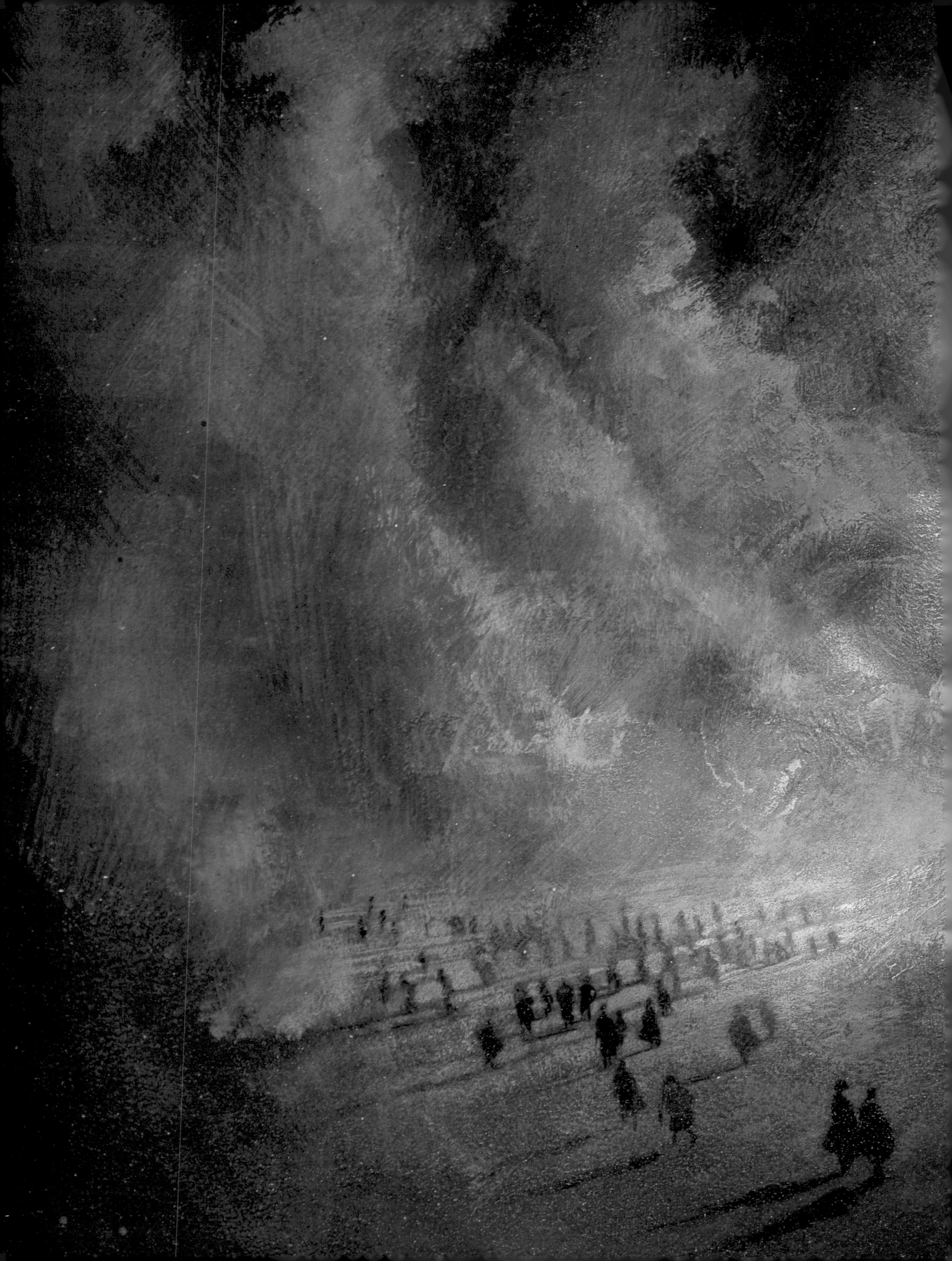

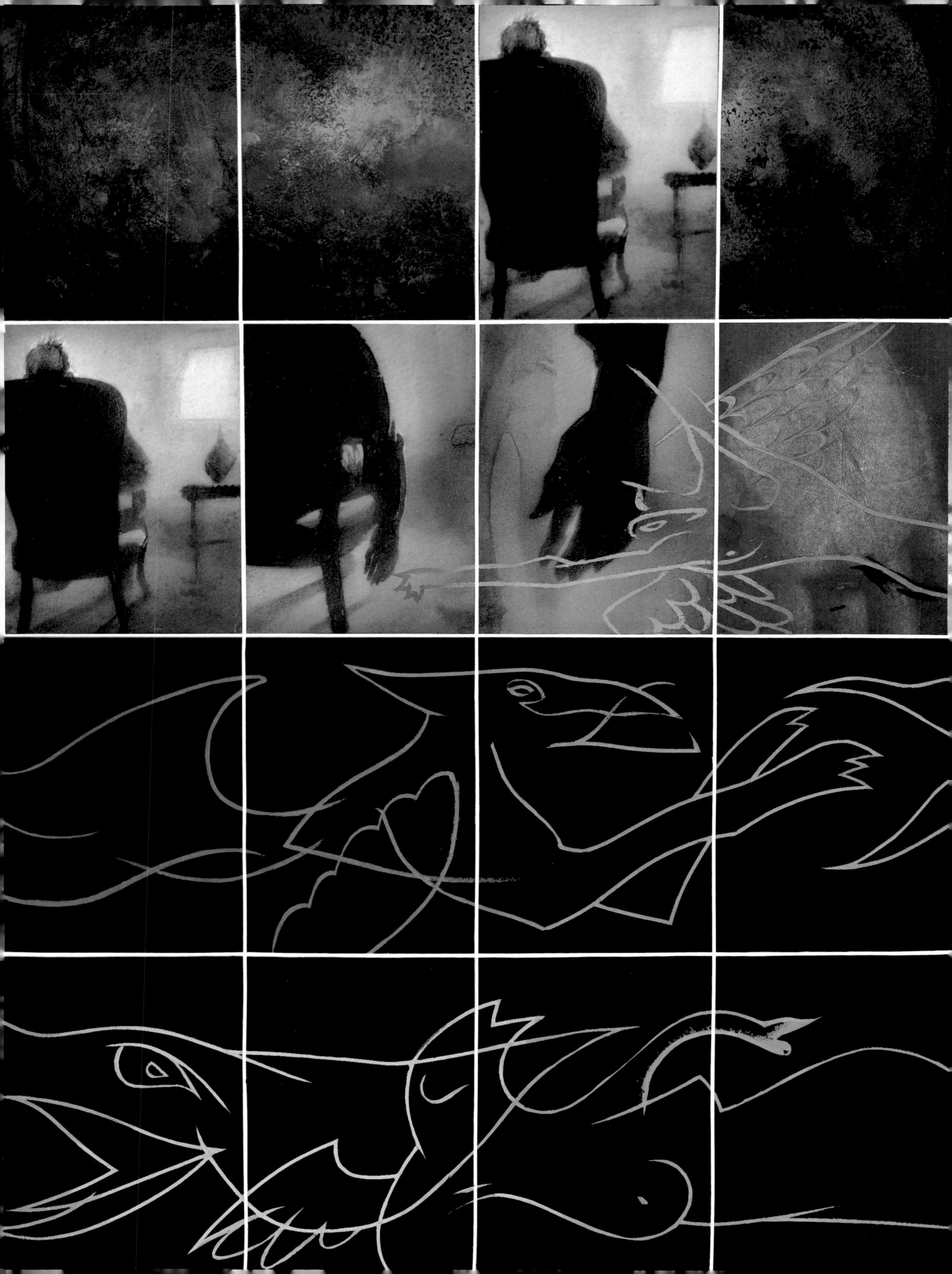

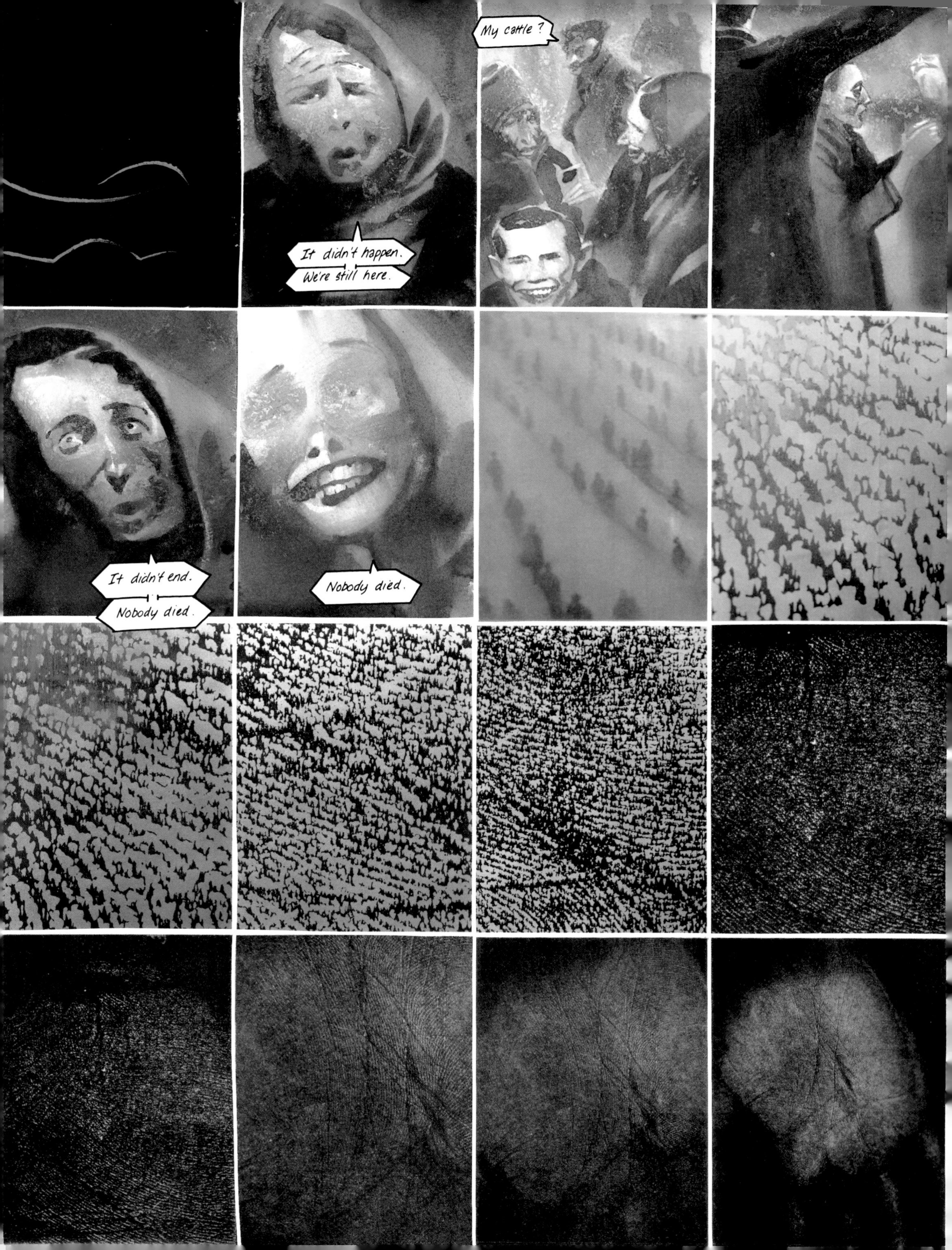
It didn't happen.
We're still here.
My cattle?
It didn't end.
Nobody died.
Nobody died.

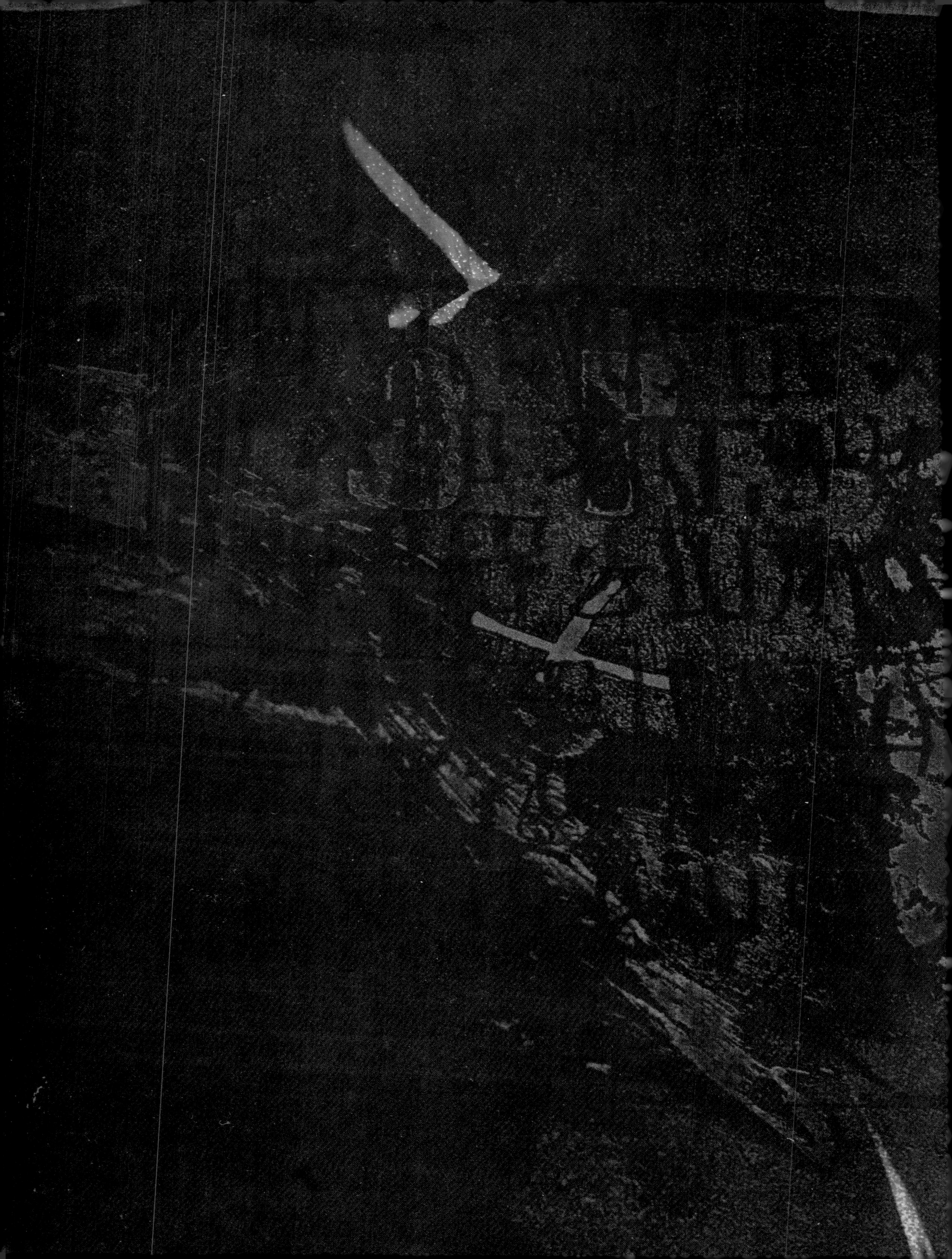

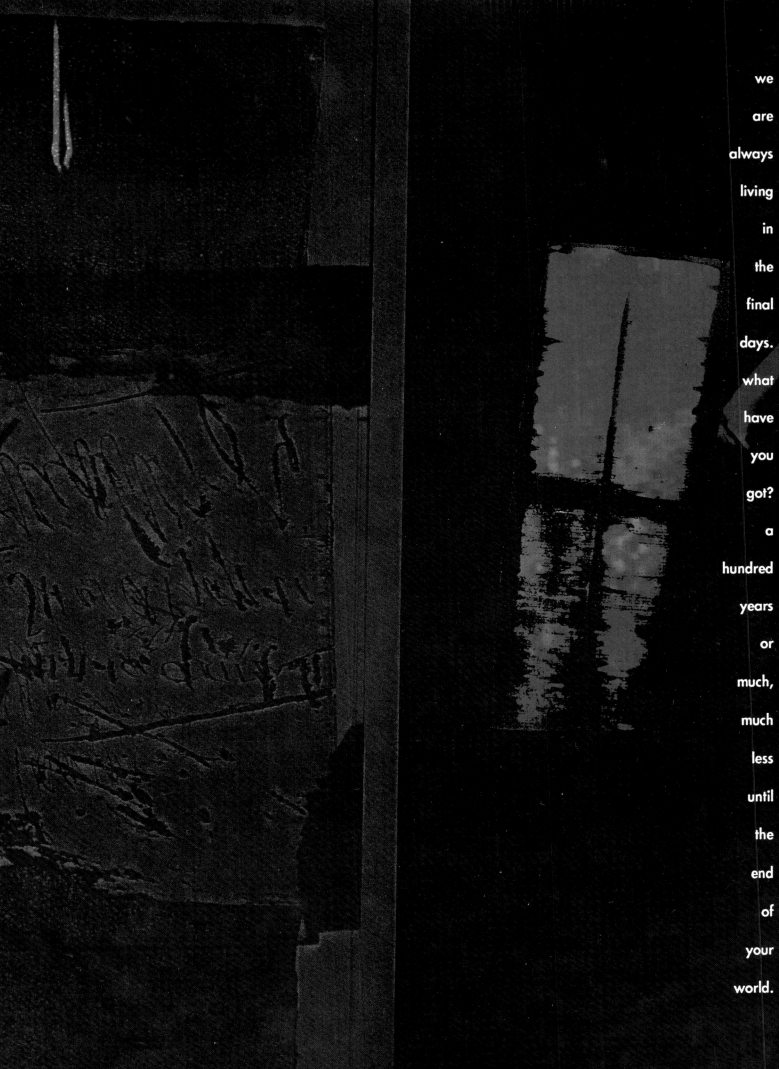

we

are

always

living

in

the

final

days.

what

have

you

got?

a

hundred

years

or

much,

much

less

until

the

end

of

your

world.

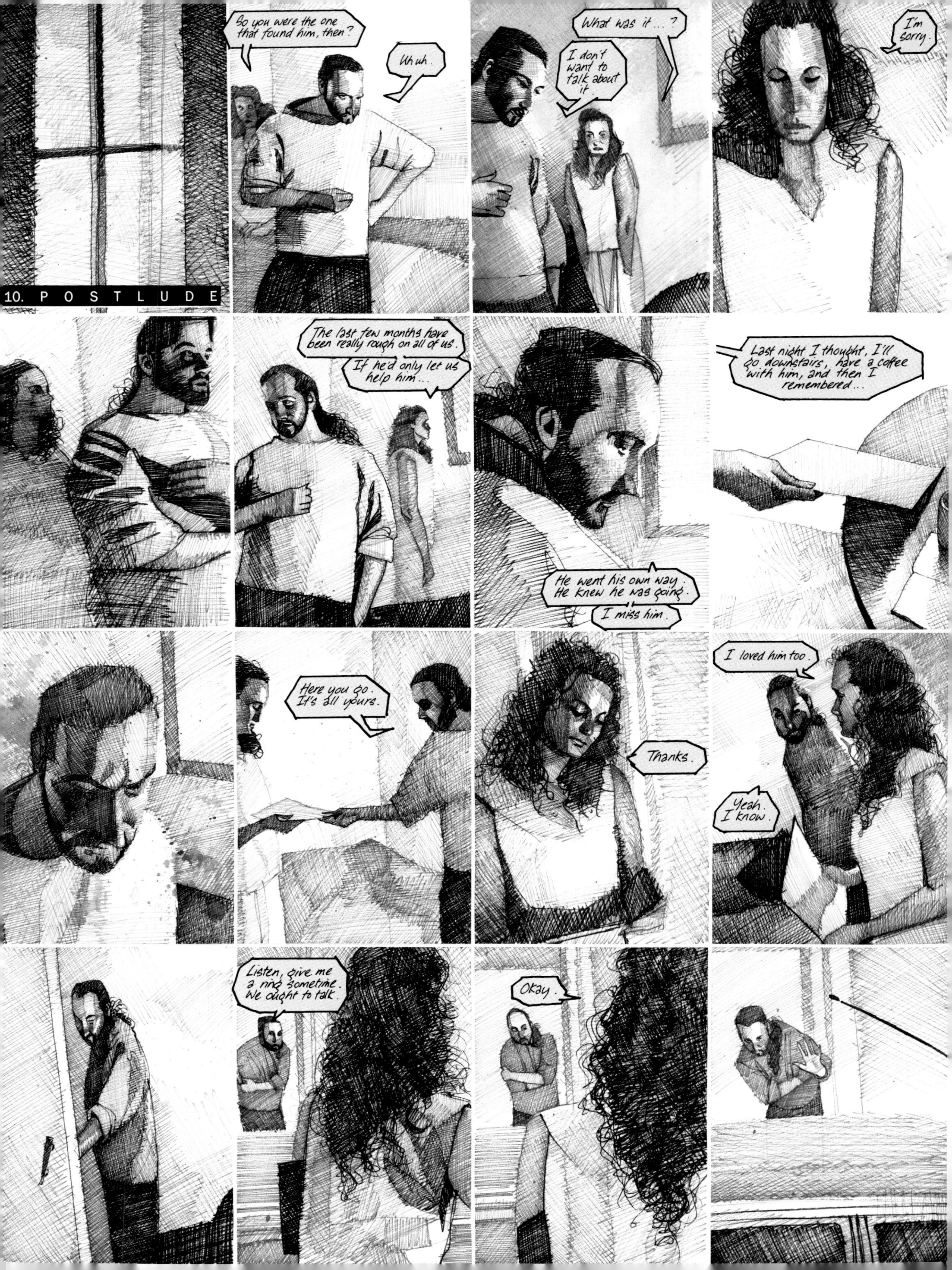
10. POSTLUDE
So you were the one that found him, then?
Uh uh.
What was it ...?
I don't want to talk about it.
I'm sorry.
The last few months have been really rough on all of us.
If he'd only let us help him...
He went his own way. He knew he was going.
I miss him.
Last night I thought, I'll go downstairs, have a coffee with him, and then I remembered...
Here you go. It's all yours.
Thanks.
I loved him too.
Yeah. I know.
Listen, give me a ring sometime. We ought to talk.
Okay.

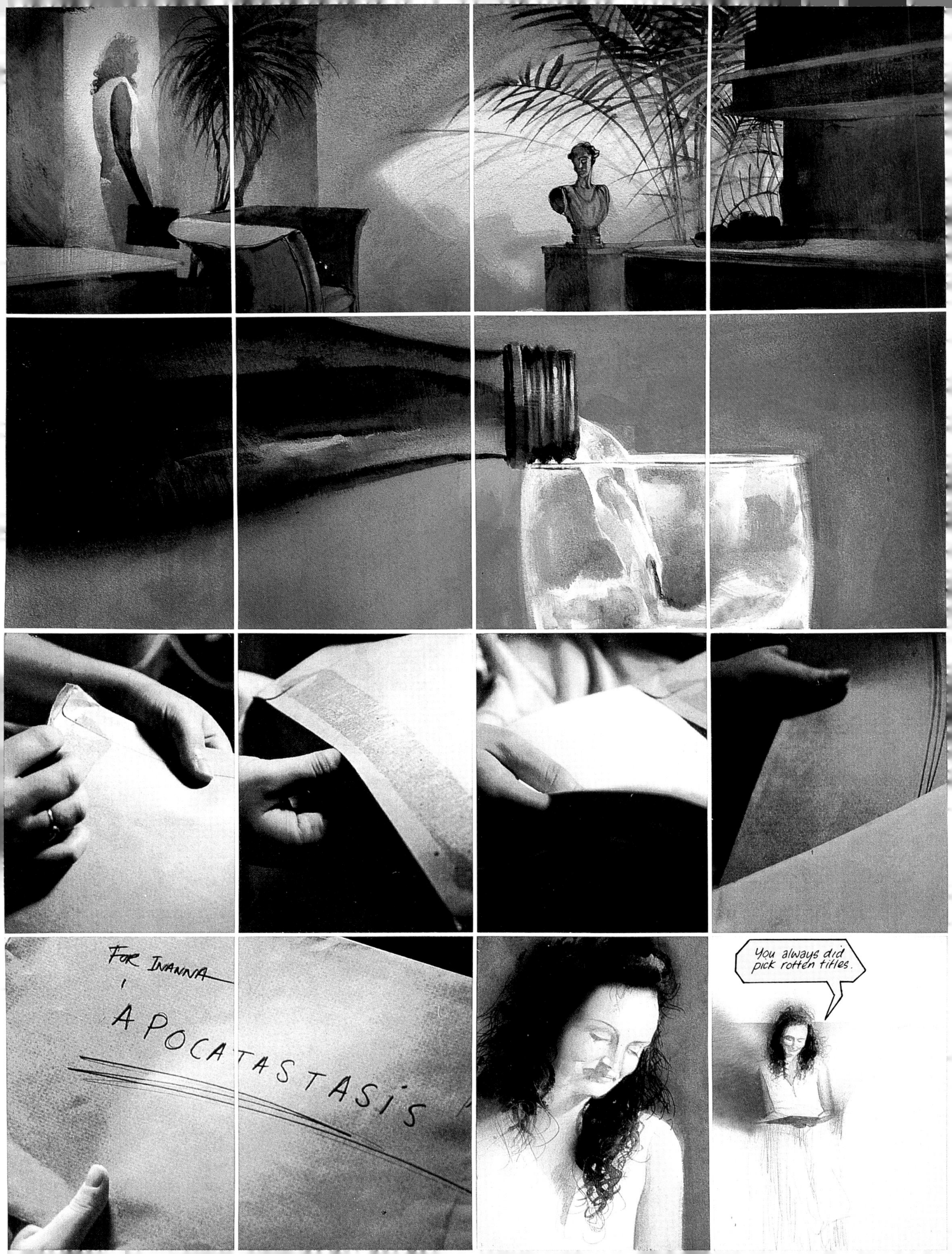
FOR INANNA
APOCATASTASIS
You always did pick rotten titles.

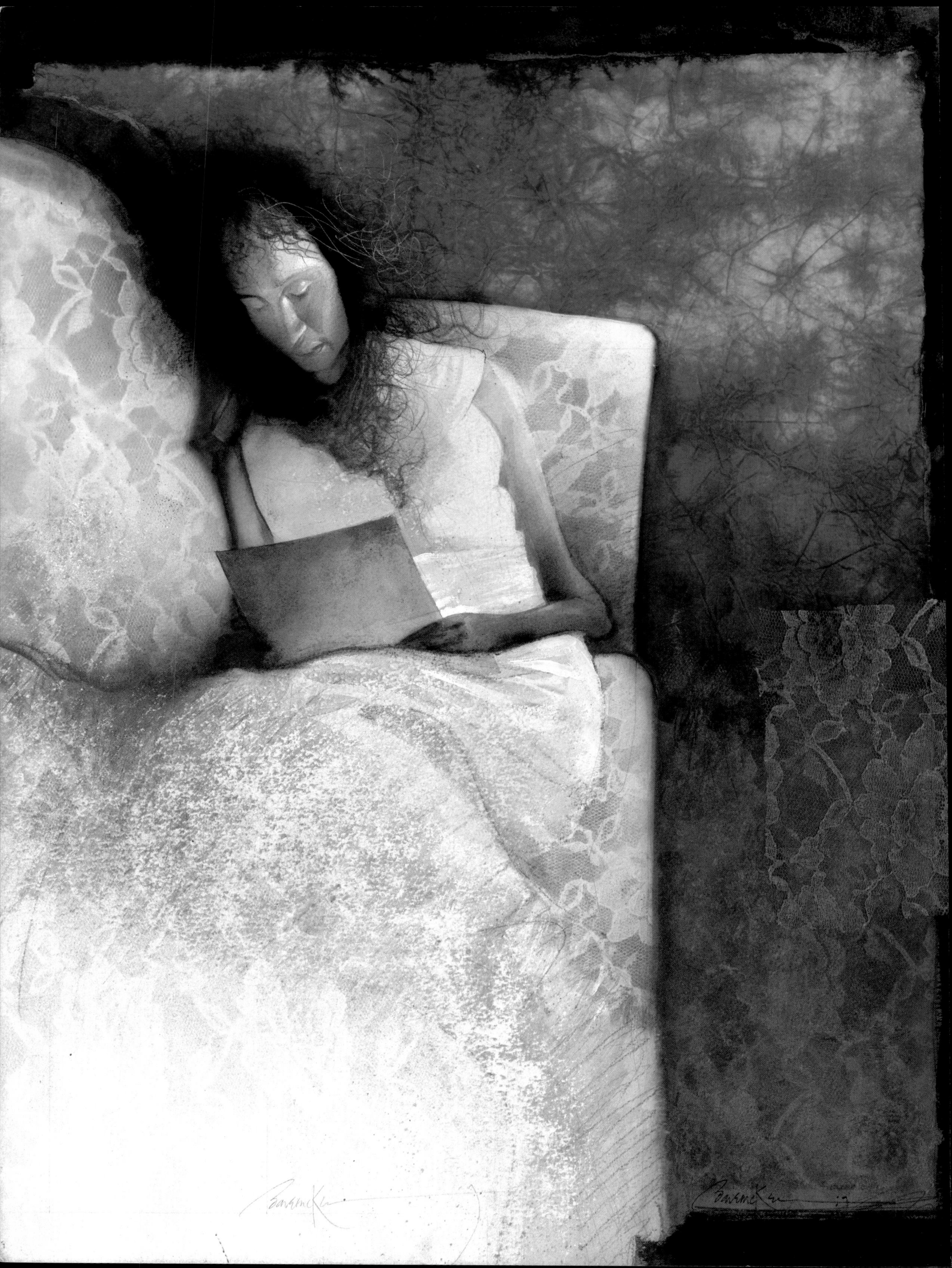

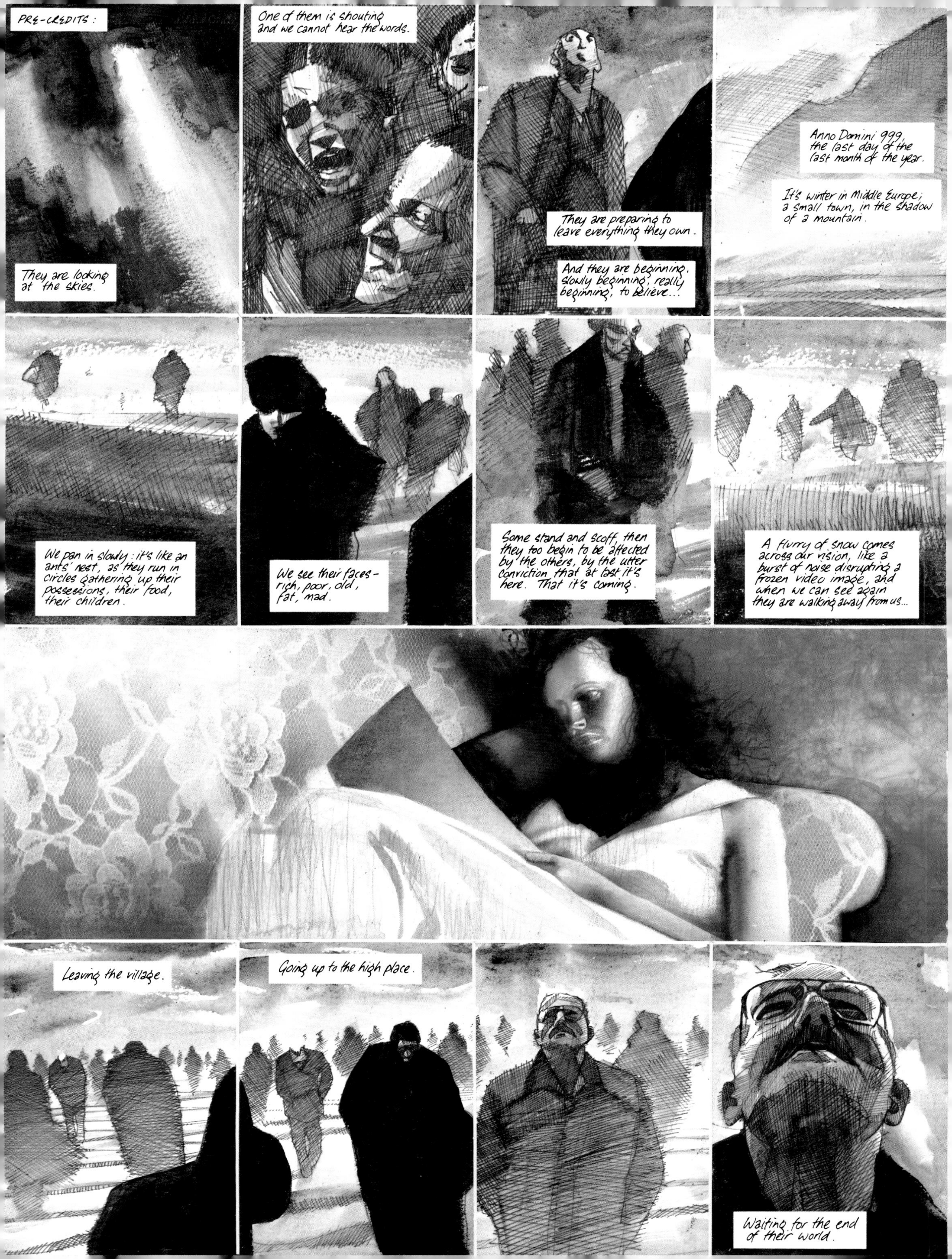
PRE-CREDITS:
They are looking at the skies.
One of them is shouting and we cannot hear the words.
They are preparing to leave everything they own.
And they are beginning, slowly beginning, really beginning, to believe...
Anno Domini 999, the last day of the last month of the year.
It's winter in Middle Europe; a small town, in the shadow of a mountain.
We pan in slowly: it's like an ants' nest, as they run in circles gathering up their possessions, their food, their children.
We see their faces - rich, poor, old, fat, mad.
Some stand and scoff, then they too begin to be affected by the others, by the utter conviction that at last it's here. That it's coming.
A flurry of snow comes across our vision, like a burst of noise disrupting a frozen video image, and when we can see again they are walking away from us...
Leaving the village.
Going up to the high place.
Waiting for the end of their world.

Intertextual material was
created with the assistance
of a Canon Lasercopier
3000, and the Babble 2.0
text sampler programme.

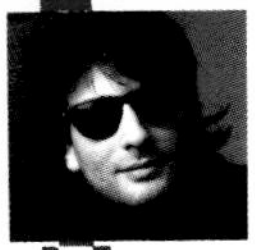

Neil Gaiman was born on the 10th of November 1960. His work in comics includes *Violent Cases*, the ten volumes of *Sandman*, and *Mr Punch*. His novels include *Neverwhere* (also a BBC TV series), *Stardust*, and approximately 50% of *Good Omens*. He has been honoured with many awards from all over the world, and you'd think it would have settled him down a bit, but he still goes to bed long after his bedtime and probably always will.

He wrote the script for the 1996 Radio 3 adaptation of *Signal to Noise*, but had nothing to do with the recent theatrical version. (*Photo: M. C. Valada*)

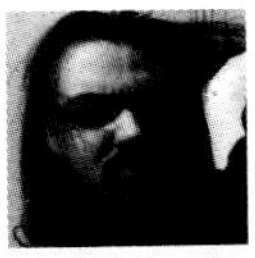

Dave McKean has illustrated many comics and graphic novels, including *Mr Punch, Arkham Asylum, Slow Chocolate Autopsy, Voodoo Lounge* and *Cages*. He produced all the covers and design for Neil's award-winning *Sandman* series. Dave has also illustrated well over 100 CDs for Michael Nyman, Tori Amos, Fear Factory, Bill Bruford, Alice Cooper, FLA and many others. He recently collaborated with John Cale on his autobiography, *What's Welsh For Zen*, and with Iain Sinclair and Chris Pettit on the award-winning film *The Falconer*. Dave's own film *The Week Before* is currently doing the rounds of festivals in Europe and the US. He lives and works in Kent, England.

r travelers, every now and then you'll see a house with windows boarded over, and bo